JN111836

Critical Thinking through Authentic Video

Expanding

**CEFR
A1-A2**

■ 世界を巡る映像で学ぶ総合英語〈基礎〉

Horizons

Charles Browne 田邉祐司

NAN'UN-DO

映像
ストリーミング

ビデオ映像
無料視聴
のご案内

このテキストのビデオ映像を無料で視聴（ストリーミング）できます。
自習用としてご活用ください。
以下のサイトにアクセスしてテキスト番号で検索してください。

https://nanun-do.com　テキスト番号 [**512044**]

※ 無線 LAN（WiFi）に接続してのご利用を推奨いたします。ストリーミング再生
では、動画ファイルは保存されません。再生する度にデータをインターネット経
由で読み込みますので、通信量にご注意ください。

※ キャリア回線を使用する場合、お使いのキャリアの料金プラン等によっては、
高額なインターネット通信料金が発生する場合がありますのでご注意ください。

※ Expanding Horizons【CEFR A1-A2】映像視聴ページは以下の
QR コードからもご利用になれます。

Foreword

Welcome to *Expanding Horizons: Critical Thinking through Authentic Video*.

It has long been known that one of the most important factors in developing English language skills over time is regular, daily exposure to input in English that is both at an appropriate level, as well as of personal interest to the learner. *Expanding Horizons: Critical Thinking through Authentic Video* is a 4-skills book that is designed to help you improve your English skills through exposure to authentic, award-winning videos that are carefully graded to follow the CEFR framework, as well as to original, high-interest readings, also carefully graded to CEFR level. The first half of the book, units 1-7 have videos, texts and activities that are at the A1 level, and the second half of the book, units 8-14, are at the low-A2 level.

Although input is an essential starting point for language learning it is not enough – regular, daily output, too, is crucial if you want to be able to advance beyond the beginner level. *Expanding Horizons* addresses this by taking a strong student-centered approach, which gives lots of opportunities for you to discuss and share your ideas, experiences and opinions with other students in English, using language in ways that will that encourages the development of critical thinking skills. We have tried to strike a balance between fluency-oriented writing and paired/group activities (meaning you don't have to worry about making mistakes in English), and accuracy-focused shadowing, dictation/dictogloss and vocabulary development activities that will help improve your pronunciation, listening and speaking skills.

We believe that English language learning materials as well as the learning experience itself should be interesting, easy and fun and have done our best to make Expanding Horizons exactly that. We hope that you will enjoy studying English with this book and that it will help you to expand your horizons!

Dr. Charles Browne
Dr. Yuji Tanabe

1. **WARM UP: Talk about it**

   This activity is picture-based and designed to activate your real-world knowledge on the topic of the unit.

2. **VOCABULARY: Matching**

   This activity teaches the most important vocabulary words needed to understand the contents of the video. Definitions are given in easy English and match the meanings given in the video.

3. **VIDEO: Predicting**

   This activity usually asks you to make some predictions about what you think the video might be about. It helps draw you into the video as well as activate your knowledge on the topic. (Schema building)

4. **VIDEO: Listening for Specific Information**

   There are several types of activities in this section, all of which can be characterized as "while-listening" activities, designed to help you to listen more actively and comprehend the video more fully.

5. **LISTENING: Comprehension**

   These are more standard comprehension-style questions designed to make sure whether or not you understand the key points of the video.

6. **Dictogloss**

   You will work together with other students to try to reconstruct key sentences from the video before listening to check your answers.

7. **Focus on Grammar**

   This video dictation activity is an awareness-raising activity designed to focus your attention on one of the key grammar points of the lesson, specifically as to how this grammar is used in authentic, natural English speech.

8. **DISCUSSION**

   This is a student-centered speaking activity designed to help you to think more deeply about the video, and to begin to communicate and share your ideas and opinions with others about this topic.

9. **WRITING: Critical Thinking**

   This activity is designed to help you to think more deeply about the topic as well as to move from an input-focus (the video and readings) to a more output-focus. This is done by asking you to write your ideas on the topic, which will also help you with the speaking activities later in the unit.

10. QUOTABLE QUOTES

This picture-based activity introduces a quote, usually from a famous person, that is related to the topic of the unit. It is designed to help you to think deeply about the topic you have been studying.

11. VOICE DICTION: Video Shadowing

The dictation part of this activity gives you practice in developing your intensive listening skills while the shadowing part of the activity helps you to work on and improve your pronunciation, especially at the sentence level.

12. ROLE PLAYING: Natural Speech

This activity encourages you to communicate in natural English based on situations introduced in the video and the whole unit.

13. CRITICAL DISCUSSION

This activity builds on the writing activity given earlier in the unit, providing you with a real audience for your writing as well as a chance to discuss and think more critically about the topic at hand.

14. READING

This is a short original reading that relates to the topic of the unit. It is written in easy English with a controlled vocabulary, designed both to give more information and a different point of view on the topic of the unit as well as to provide an authentic context for the grammar point of the unit.

15. SPEAKING

This is a more open-ended speaking activity designed to allow you to talk about interesting ideas and topics related to the unit, but with a semi-structured pre-speaking activity to help you get started.

16. WRITING: Let's Brainstorm and Go!!

This is a paired writing activity, encouraging you to share ideas as well as to help/teach each other the language needed to complete the activity. Like the previous writing activity, this one assumes your classmates will be the audience for the writing, which should help you to focus on writing in a way that will lead to fruitful/interesting discussions.

17. OPTIONAL PROJECTS: Group and Individual

Each unit provides at least 1-2 additional, optional projects should you want to extend the lesson or dig more deeply into the topic. Often the projects culminate with presenting the results to the class in the form of a Powerpoint, a poster or some kind of presentation, while encouraging the audience to actively ask follow-up questions.

Contents

Unit 1
The Sky Lodge: An Unusual Hotel <Holidays>

Learning Goals	Vocabulary and Grammar in the Video

Practical English:
  ● Speaking: Talking about unusual holidays
  ● Listening: Inferring meaning from context
 	
Critical Thinking:
  ● Why do people like to stay in unusual places?
	Vocabulary:
	  ● Common Adjectives
	  ● Routines
	
	Grammar:
	  ● Simple Past
	  ● Adjectives Expressing Emotion

WARM UP: Talk about it

Work with a partner and answer the questions below.

- Who are the people in the picture?

- What do you think they are doing?

- Where do you think they are?

VOCABULARY: Matching

Match the words and phrases (1-8) to their definitions (a-h).

1. cool   _____   a. to arrive at

2. scary   _____   b. low in temperature, but not cold, often in a way that feels pleasant

3. amazing   _____   c. to begin to sleep

4. zipline   _____   d. very good, especially in an unexpected way

5. cliff   _____   e. a strong wire going from a high place to a lower place, with a pulley hanging from it. People hold onto the pulley and travel along the wire, usually for fun

6. at night   _____   f. a mountain with a very steep side, often at the edge of the sea or a river

7. fall asleep   _____   g. after it gets dark

8. get to   _____   h. frightening

VIDEO: Predicting

Before watching the video, try to answer the following questions.

1. What do you think The Sky Lodge is?

_____   _____

2. Where do you think it might be?

_____

Now watch the video and check your answers. Who was the closest?

VIDEO: Sequencing

Work with a partner. Look at the sentences below and discuss what you think the correct order is. Compare your answers with another pair. Then watch the video to check your answers.

_____ You leave The Sky Lodge by zipline.

_____ The Sky Lodge is a hotel in Peru.

_____ You should visit The Sky Lodge if you like mountains and a good view.

_____ Tony and Thomas can't sleep because the view from the hotel is so beautiful.

_____ To get to The Sky Lodge, you have to climb a mountain.

_____ In the morning, Tony and Thomas go to a different room to have breakfast.

LISTENING: Comprehension

Watch again. Circle T for True and F for False.

1. Thomas and Tony are in Chile.　　　　T　F

2. The hotel has glass walls.　　　　T　F

3. They eat dinner outside.　　　　T　F

4. They leave by taking ziplines.　　　　T　F

Dictogloss

Fill in the blanks by talking with your partners. Then watch the video to check your answers.

1. They're visiting Peru, and (　　　　　　) in a hotel that's 1,200 feet
   (　　　　　　　) the ground! (0:22)

2. The hotel (　　　　　) (　　　　　　　) The Sky Lodge. (0:29)

3. Going (　　　　　) (　　　　　　) (　　　　　　) hotel isn't easy,
   but it's very exciting. (0:50)

4. I don't (　　　　　) (　　　　　　) asleep! This is (　　　　　)
   the most (　　　　　　) hotel stay of my life and ... I don't want to sleep! (1:35)

Focus on Adjectives

Thomas describes his feelings (2:41). Listen and fill in the blanks.

This is so _____ and _____ and _____ ...

DISCUSSION

Make a small group and discuss the following questions.

1. Would you like to stay in The Sky Lodge? Why or why not?

2. Have you heard of any other unusual places to stay? Where? What is unusual about it?

3. What is the most unusual vacation you/family/friends have experienced?

WRITING: Critical Thinking

Do you like traveling? Why do you think people like to stay in places like The Sky Lodge? Write a short essay with your opinion and bring it to class next time.

QUOTABLE QUOTES: Warm up

"To travel is to live ..."

Look at the quote above. Think about this unit. What do you think the quote means?

VOICE DICTION: Video Shadowing

Start the video at 0:12 and (video counter) play one sentence by the narrator.

1) Fill in the blank with the missing words.

Tony and Thomas write (   ) (   ).

2) Watch the scenes and pronounce at the same time. Repeat several times until you can do it smoothly.

ROLE PLAYING: Natural Speech

Work with a partner. Watch the scenes below. Pause the video at each place. Then role play what you would say if you were Tony or Thomas in that scene. Use the language box to help you.

- 00:40 Tony about to climb the mountain

- 01:02 Tony climbing into the room

- 01:26 Tony and Thomas looking outside

- 02:00 Tony and Thomas having breakfast

- 02:20 Thomas going down on the zipline

LANGUAGE BOX

- **Wow! This is scary!**
- **I can't do it!**
- **What an amazing view!**

CRITICAL DISCUSSION

Make groups of 3-4 students. Read each essay one by one. For each essay:

- Write one question you would like to ask the writer.
- Write one suggestion to help them improve the essay.

Now, answer some of the questions. Your teacher may ask you to rewrite and expand your essay.

READING: Awareness Raising - Simple Past

Find and correct the 10 errors in the essay below. Then listen to the CD to check your answers.

I love traveling. My parents take me to many different countries when I was young. I see many beautiful and famous sights such as the Eiffel Tower and Louvre Museum in Paris, the Grand Canyon and the Statue of Liberty in the US and Big Ben and Buckingham Palace in London. ₅ But more enjoyable than all of these is a trip I took to Mongolia as a college student. My teacher try to teach us about poverty and social problems in other countries. But being from such a rich and comfortable country as Japan, at first I cannot relate to what he was trying to teach us. As part of the class, we had to identify a ₁₀ problem in a different country and then go to that country to do volunteer work to try and help fix that problem. In this case, our class find out there was a terrible housing

problem in Mongolia and we decide to go there to help build houses through a group called Habitat for Humanity. Working together with local people, in just 2 weeks my class can build 7 houses! Although it was very hard work and we didn't get to see many famous sites, I loved my trip to Mongolia because I learn many things, helped many people and made many special friendships. ₁₅ ₂₀

SPEAKING

Think of 2 interesting places you visited. Why did you enjoy it? One example has been given for you.

Place	Reasons
(e.g.) Mongolia	Because we could make friends with many local people by working together with them.

Make a small group. Introduce all the places you went and vote on the most exciting one. Then choose a spokesperson to introduce it to the class.

WRITING: Let's Brainstorm and Go!!

With your partner, discuss your dream vacation. Where would you like to go? What would you like to do? After that, write it down your whole plan and use your notes to present to another pair.

Place we would like to go: _____

	Notes
Things to do	
Things to see	
Things to eat	
How to get there	
Where to stay	

OPTIONAL PROJECTS:

Choose one of the projects below. Be ready to show your results by next class.

Group Project: Tourism

Make a group. Discuss what you liked and disliked about the Sky Lodge. Then work together to design a guide for tourists, preparing them for their stay. Your guide should include ideas for what to pack, what to prepare for, and what to be excited about.

Individual Project: V-Log

Think of an exciting holiday you took. Imagine you are on the holiday and record yourself saying short vlog-style sentences describing it. (e.g. "Here I am at the top of the volcano. It's really, really hot here but the sunrise is beautiful!.") Then watch the vlogs made by everyone and vote for the one that sounds most exciting.

CEFR GOALS SELF- EVALUATION	
I can talk about unusual holidays.	1---2---3---4---5
I can infer meaning from context.	1---2---3---4---5
I understand common routines.	1---2---3---4---5
I can use the simple past tense.	1---2---3---4---5
I can use adjectives expressing emotions.	1---2---3---4---5
I can clearly state my opinion about dream vacations.	1---2---3---4---5

Unit 2
Japanese High School Life <School>

Learning Goals	Vocabulary and Grammar in the Video
Practical English: • Speaking: Talking about familiar topics like school life in a different context • Listening: Inferring meaning of phrasal verbs from context Critical Thinking: • Considering whether school rules are necessary	Vocabulary: • Words and Phrases that are used in School • Education Grammar: • Simple Past (regular and irregular) • Time Concordance

WARM UP: Talk about it
Work with a partner and answer the questions below.

- How old do you think the girl in the picture is?
- Where do you think she is?

VOCABULARY: Matching

Match the words and phrases (1-8) to their definitions (a-h).

1. every single day _____   a. two things that are closely connected

2. go for _____   b. every day

3. take off _____   c. used to say that something is completely finished

4. go hand-in-hand with _____   d. to dislike something very much

5. That's it. _____   e. to arrive at a place

6. uniform _____   f. to try to do or complete something

7. hate _____   g. a type of clothing worn by all the members of a group

8. get to _____   h. to remove a piece of clothing

VIDEO: Predicting

Before watching the video, guess whether Sophie will mostly like or mostly dislike the school rules in Japan. Circle your guess: (mostly like/mostly dislike)

Next, fill in the chart below while watching the video and then check your answers.

Sophie loved ...	Sophie hated ...

VIDEO: Sequencing

Work with a partner. Look at the sentences below and discuss what you think the correct order is. Compare your answers with another pair. Then watch the video to check your answers.

_____ Sophie does not like the idea of students' cleaning the classroom.

_____ Sophie is going to school by bicycle.

_____ Sophie is putting on her school uniforms.

_____ Sophie is talking about her lunch box.

_____ Sophie is taking off her shoes before entering a school building.

FUN FACT Please note that English is not Sophie's first language and that she sometimes makes small errors. This is less important than how easy and clear her English is. "Communicative Ability" means being able to make your message easily understood — we think you will agree that Sophie does this wonderfully!

LISTENING: Comprehension

Watch again. Circle T for True and F for False.

1. Sophie wears her school uniform when she goes to school.   T   F

2. Sophie doesn't like the cleaning of the classroom.   T   F

3. Sophie has to take off her shoes when entering the school.   T   F

4. Sophie has lunch at school cafeteria.   T   F

Dictogloss

Fill in the blanks by talking with your partners. Then watch the video to check your answers.

1. I (   ) loved riding my bicycle to school every (   ) day. (0:48)

2. So, that doesn't only (   ) for (   ) in Japan, it also goes (   ) a lot of public buildings (   ) schools! (1:08)

3. The third thing I really loved about my Japanese high school, and it (   ) (   ) hand-in-hand with the shoes (   ), was my school uniform. (1:58)

4. I don't really think I (   ) to (   ) that, because food is the best, right? (2:17)

Focus on Time Concordance

Sophie talks about her favorite things about Japanese high school (1:01). Listen and fill in the blanks.

Number two of the things that I _____ in my Japanese high school _____ that you _____ actually allowed to wear shoes inside of the building.

DISCUSSION

Sophie loved the following 3 things about Japanese high schools. In pairs, discuss if you agree with her opinion or not. Say why for each one.

1. Wearing a school uniform

2. Not wearing shoes in school

3. Cleaning the classroom at the end of every day

WRITING: Critical Thinking

Think about when you went to high school. Where there any rules you disliked? Why? Write a short essay with your opinion and bring it to class next time.

QUOTABLE QUOTES: Warm up

"Education is the most powerful weapon which you can use to change the world."
By Nelson Mandela

Look at the quote above. Think about this unit. What do you think it means?

VOICE DICTION: Video Shadowing

Start the video at 1:13 and play one sentence by the narrator.

1) Fill in the blank with the missing words.

So basically (   ) you enter (   ) Japanese high school, or probably any school, there is a place (   ) everyone takes off (   ) shoes.

2) Watch the scenes and pronounce at the same time. Repeat several times until you can do it smoothly.

ROLE PLAYING: Natural Speech

Work with a partner. Watch the scenes below. Pause the video at each place. Then role play what you would say if you were Sophie in that scene. Use the language box to help you.

- 00:16 Sophie introducing herself

- 00:47 Sophie explaining how to go to school

- 01:59 Sophie explaining her school uniform

- 02:11 Sophie explaining the bento

- 02:45 Sophie finishing the video

LANGUAGE BOX

- **I was super excited to ...**
- **It's the absolute best.**
- **I'm serious!**

CRITICAL DISCUSSION

Make groups of 3-4 students. Read each essay one by one. For each essay:

- Write one question you would like to ask the writer.
- Write one suggestion to help them improve the essay.

Now, answer some of the questions. Your teacher may ask you to rewrite and expand your essay.

READING: Awareness Raising – Time Concordance

This is what Sophie wrote about her life in Japan. Find and correct the 5 tense errors in the essay below. Then listen to the CD to check your answers.

Hi Amelia,

How've you been doing? Sorry for this belated email. I've been too busy to  find time to write to you. Let me describe my life here. It's been almost one month since I settle down here. The city was located at the foot of ⁵ Mt. Fuji, which is the highest mountain in Japan. I now live with a Japanese family. They are really good people. They have a beautiful dog named Niko. He is an American Labradoodle and so much fun to play with - I've taken him to the park ¹⁰ near the lake almost every day and go running with him. He loves to play fetch the ball!

School is also a lot of fun. I need to ride my bicycle about 2 km to got there but the area is so pretty that I look forward to my rides. I was surprised to find out that students and teachers are not allowed to wear shoes in the school. I ¹⁵ guess that helps to keep the place clean. Anyhow, I miss you and look forward to see you again when I get back.

Sincerely,

Sophie

SPEAKING

Think of 2 things you like in your school life. Why do you like them? One example has been given for you.

Philosophy	Reasons
(e.g.) School uniform	Because I wear a uniform, I don't have to choose my clothes every day.

Make a small group. Introduce all the things you like in your school life and vote on the most interesting one. Then choose a spokesperson to introduce it to the class.

WRITING: Let's Brainstorm and Go!!

With your partner, discuss school rules. Are they necessary? Choose one and discuss its advantages or disadvantages? After that, write down your opinion and use your notes to present to another pair.

The school rule we chose: _____

	Notes
Explanation of the rule	
Our opinion	*necessary/unnecessary (circle one)*
Reasons	1) 2) 3)

OPTIONAL PROJECTS:

Choose one of the projects below. Be ready to show your results by next class.

Group Project: Ideal School

Make a group. Discuss what kind of school or school life is ideal for you. Then work together to design a school advertisement for applicants. Your advertisement should include school name, location, how to go to school and school rules.

Individual Project: Vlog

Think of what you loved about your high school or high school life. Imagine you are at school and record yourself saying short vlog-style sentences describing your favorites. (E.g. "Hey, everyone. What I loved about my school was its school cafeteria".) Then watch the v-logs made by everyone and vote for the one that sounds most exciting.

CEFR GOALS SELF- EVALUATION	
I can talk about school life in a different context.	1---2---3---4---5
I can infer meaning of phrasal verbs from context.	1---2---3---4---5
I understand cultural difference.	1---2---3---4---5
I can use the simple past tense.	1---2---3---4---5
I can use time concordance.	1---2---3---4---5
I can clearly state my opinion about school rules.	1---2---3---4---5

Unit 3
Sloth Calendar <Nature>

Learning Goals	Vocabulary and Grammar in the Video
Practical English: • Speaking: talking about cute animals • Listening: inferring meaning from context Critical Thinking: • Thinking about what is important in life	Vocabulary: • Nature • Verbs (things animals do) Grammar: • Present Simple (third person singular) • Determiners: a, every, other, another

WARM UP: Talk about it

Look at the picture above. Work with a partner and answer the questions below.

- Have you ever seen this animal in the zoo or on TV/the Internet?
- What characteristics do we associate with this animal?

VOCABULARY: Matching

Match the words and phrases (1-8) to their definitions (a-h).

1. sloth _____   a. animals that live in nature by themselves

2. savior _____   b. not sleeping

3. to hide _____   c. an animal that moves very slowly, has grey fur, and lives in trees

4. awake _____   d. to be inactive or not moving for a long time

5. sanctuary _____   e. someone who saves you from a difficult or dangerous situation

6. to feed _____   f. to go or stay in a place where no one will see or find you

7. wild _____   g. an area for birds or animals where they are protected

8. to do nothing _____   h. to give food to a person or animal

VIDEO: Predicting

Review the title of this unit and the first picture, then try to guess the answers to the questions below:

1. Where do you think the video takes place?

_____

2. What job does the person in the video have?

_____

Now watch the video and check your answers with a partner. Who was closest to being right?

VIDEO: Sequencing

Work with a partner. Look at the sentences below and discuss what you think the correct order is. Compare your answers with another pair. Then watch the video to check your answers.

_____ The best place to take cute sloth pictures is the Baby Sloth sanctuary.

_____ Lucy's calendar has the message "relax and take life easy".

_____ The sloth called Jon Snow woke up for about 5 minutes.

_____ The mother and baby sloths are hiding in the trees.

_____ Sloths sleep all the time.

LISTENING: Comprehension

Watch again. Circle T for True and F for False.

1. Sam Trull said that Lucy has a great job.   T   F

2. Every year Lucy travels to the forest in Costa Rica.   T   F

3. Wild sloths are easy to find because they like people.   T   F

4. Lucy uses a whistle to make sloths wake up.   T   F

Dictogloss

Fill in the blanks by talking with your partners. Then watch the video to check your answers.

1. She (   ) to the forest in Costa Rica to (   ) the sloths
   for her sloth calendar. (0:33)

2. They're (   ) and like to (   ). (0:56)

3. Jon Snow (   ) (   ) for about five minutes to
   (   ) me his handsome (   ). (1:47)

4. Sam shows Lucy the best place for (   ) and very (   )
   sloth photos: the (   ) Sloth Sanctuary. (1:59)

Focus on Determiners

The Narrator is talking about what Lucy and Sam are doing (1:02). Listen and fill in the blanks.

Now, Lucy and Sam are looking for _____ _____ and _____
_____. They are hiding in the trees. But sometimes, the photos are not very
good. Lucy needs to find _____ _____ for January.

DISCUSSION

Make a small group and discuss the following questions.

1. Where is the best place to take cute sloth photos?
2. Why does Lucy whistle with a D sharp tone?
3. What message does Lucy's calendar have?

WRITING: Critical Thinking

How can trying to be more like a sloth help you in your daily life? Write a short essay with your
opinion and bring it to class next time.

QUOTABLE QUOTES: Warm up

"Don't underestimate the value of doing nothing, of just going along, listening to all the things you can't hear, and not bothering."
By A.A. Milne, author of Winne the Pooh

Look at the quote above. Think about the life of a sloth. What do you think it means?

VOICE DICTION: Video Shadowing

Start the video at 1:13 and play one sentence by the narrator.

1) Fill in the blank with the missing words.

(   ) (   ), the photos (   ) not very good.

2) Watch the scenes and pronounce at the same time. Repeat several times until you can do it smoothly.

ROLE PLAYING: Natural Speech

Work with a partner. Watch the scenes below. Pause the video at the end of each section. Then role play what you would say if you were Lucy in that scene. Use the language box to help you.

- 01:00-01:24 Lucy was looking for a sloth, and finally found one

- 01:29-01:56 Lucy found Jon Snow awake for about five minutes

- 01:58-02:22 Lucy taking photographs of sloths

LANGUAGE BOX

- **This is a super sloth saviour.**
- **Just long enough for me to ...**
- **Put on a good show.**

CRITICAL DISCUSSION

Make groups of 3-4 students. Read each essay one by one. For each essay:

- Write one question you would like to ask the writer.
- Write one suggestion to help them improve the essay.

Now, answer some of the questions. Your teacher may ask you to rewrite and expand your essay.

READING: Awareness Raising - Determiners

Underline the determiners "a," "one," "another," "every" and "other" in the essay below. Then listen to the CD to check your answers.

I think that doing nothing is actually one of the most important things you can do. Our parents, our teachers and our bosses are always trying to convince us that work and working hard is the most important thing. "Another day, another dollar" is their philosophy. Even on vacations, most of the people I know are far too busy, rushing from one place to another, every day trying to squeeze in as many activities as possible. 5 I don't agree with this philosophy at all. In fact my philosophy of life, if it can be called that, is to "stop and smell the roses".

"Couch potato"? Gladly! "Sloth"? Guilty as charged! For me, one of the most important things is to try to slow down and take the time to appreciate the people, events and things around you. For example, on a beautiful sunny day at my university last week, I 10 saw people rushing across the campus to get to their classes, talking quickly with their friends or professors, or running after a frisbee or some other kind of sport. Not a single person seemed to notice the beautiful day around them. What did I do? I walked right up to a beautiful tree in the middle of campus, put my backpack of textbooks on the grass to use as a headrest, and then laid down and looked up through the tree 15 branches at the beautiful clouds and sky. As I laid there, I felt a wonderful sense of

 peace and happiness, I felt lucky to be a student at that school and refreshed by the brief break I took. I still got to class, I still finished my homework, but I did so without any feelings of stress or pressure. 20 My advice to you? Slow down and take time to smell the roses. You may get to your destination a few minutes later, but you will be far happier and content.

SPEAKING

Make a small group. Discuss your own philosophies of life. What are important things to remember if you want to be happy or successful. Why do you think so? Fill out the chart, One example has been given for you.

Philisophy	Reasons
(e.g.) Laugh at everything	It helps you to be positive, even in bad times.

Next, vote on the best idea, choose a spokesperson, and introduce it to the class.

25

WRITING: Let's Brainstorm and Go!!

With your partner, discuss the things that make you happiest. What do you like to do? Where do you like to go? Next, use your notes to present to another pair.

Things that make me happy: _____

	Notes
What do you like to do?	
Why do you like it?	
When do you feel happy?	
Where do you feel happy?	
Who do you feel happy with?	

OPTIONAL PROJECTS:

Choose one of the projects below. Be ready to show your results by next class.

Group Project: Animal Calendar

Make a group. Discuss what animal you would like to use for an animal calendar. Then work together to design an animal calendar, using photographs of the animal. Your calendar should include a message (or messages) which you think is important for our lives.

Individual Project: Show & Tell

You are going to do show and tell in the next class. The topic is "Important things for a happy life". Bring one item or photo and make a 1-minute presentation.

CEFR GOALS SELF- EVALUATION	
I can talk about one of the cutest animals in the world.	1---2---3---4---5
I can infer meaning from context.	1---2---3---4---5
I can recognize determiners in context.	1---2---3---4---5
I can use the present simple.	1---2---3---4---5
I can discuss philosophies of life.	1---2---3---4---5

Unit 4
The Skate Brothers
<Free Time>

Learning Goals	Vocabulary and Grammar in the Video
Practical English: ● Speaking: Informal speech practice ● Listening: Commenting on social media Critical Thinking: ● Why are free-time activities important?	Vocabulary: ● Free Time ● Family Grammar: ● Modals: can, could

WARM UP: Talk about it

Work with a partner and answer the questions below.

● How old do you think the boy in the picture is?

● Where do you think he is?

● What do you think this video will be about?

VOCABULARY: Matching

Match the words and phrases (1-8) to their definitions (a-h).

1. skateboarding _____   a. being enthusiastic or go to an extreme

2. cousin _____   b. a short board with wheels on either end. Young people often ride them

3. hobby _____   c. the rubber surface of a skateboard

4. skate park _____   d. the child of a person's aunt or uncle

5. longboard _____   e. a place designed for skateboarders to use

6. competition _____   f. an activity that a person does in their free time

7. crazy _____   g. a type of skateboard that is longer than others

8. grip _____   h. an event when people play against each other to try to win

VIDEO: Predicting

Work with a partner. Zion has a hobby. Think of what kinds of questions the narrator might ask him and write them down below. Compare your ideas with other pairs and add to your list.

Example: "How old are you?"

1) _____

2) _____

3) _____

Now watch the video and check your answers with a partner. Who was closest to being right?

VIDEO: Listening for Specific Information

Watch the video. Try to answer the two questions below, as well as the ones you wrote in the previous section.

1. Why did Zion start skateboarding?

_____

_____

2. What does Zion's family think of his hobby?

_____

_____

LISTENING: Comprehension

Watch again. Circle T for True and F for False.

1. Zion started to go to skate parks when he was three.   T   F

2. Zion likes to ride shortboards.   T   F

3. Jax started skating when he was two.   T   F

4. The family is not happy Zion and Jax do skateboarding.   T   F

Dictogloss - Descriptive Adjectives

Fill in the blanks by talking with your partners. Then watch the video to check your answers.

1. He is only eight years old but he is a (   ) good skater. (0:22)

2. Jax is (   ) crazy, he likes to do anything that I do, or Jagger does. (1:58)

3. The family is (   ) happy that Zion loves skateboarding so much. (2:50)

Focus on Vocabulary Related to Family.

Zion talks about how he got started on longboards (0:52). Listen and fill in the blanks.

Well, my _____ had longboards and my _____ had longboards, so I asked my _____ to get me a board.

DISCUSSION

1. Make groups of 3-4 students.

2. As a group, ask each other the following questions. Help each other to answer them.
   - Think about something you love to do in your free time. Why do you love doing it so much?
   - Do you think you could make it into something more than fun, maybe a job?

WRITING: Critical Thinking

Imagine you want to share this video with others on your favorite social media website. In the box, write a short comment to include with the video. You will show it to other students later in the unit.

USER
5 minutes ago

👍 Like   💬 Comment   ➔ Share

QUOTABLE QUOTES: Warm up

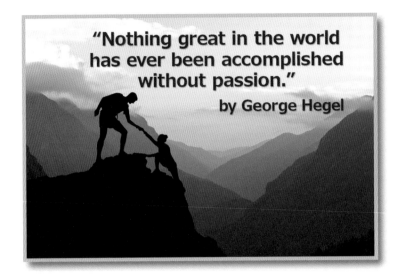

"Nothing great in the world has ever been accomplished without passion."
by George Hegel

Look at the quote above. Think about this unit. What do you think it means?

VOICE DICTION: Video Shadowing

Start the video at 1:04 (video counter) and play one sentence by Zion.
Watch the scene and pronounce at the same time. Repeat several times until you can do it smoothly.

ROLE PLAYING: Natural Speech

Work with a partner. Replay the video from 01:58 - 02:03 "Jax is really crazy! ..."

1. Repeat the sentence, copying the way that Zion says it.

2. Next, take turns making sentences about family or friends of yours that do things that are really unusual or amazing.

example:

    A: Do you have any friends that do unusual things?

    B: Yeah, my friend Justin is really crazy! He likes to jump in the river from a cliff!

CRITICAL DISCUSSION

Make groups of 3-4 students. Read each student's SMS (Social media service) post about the video. Add at least 2 comments to each one as follows:

- Write one question you would like to ask the writer.
- Write one suggestion to help them improve the essay.

Now, answer some of the questions. Your teacher may ask you to rewrite and expand your SMS post.

READING: Awareness Raising - Modals

Find and underline the 5 modals used in the essay below. Then check your answers with a partner. Then listen to the CD to check your answers.

Can you name a famous skateboarder? If you walk on the street and ask five people to name a well-known skateboarder, chances are that if they name anybody, it will be Tony Hawk. In fact, most people couldn't name a single skater other than Tony Hawk. Why?

Tony shot to fame when he became part of the Bones Brigade, the most famous skateboard team in history. He was one of the top skaters in the world by the time he was 16, has won more than 70 skateboard contest and also made many skateboard video games.

One of the first tricks intermediate skateboarders learn is called a "360", where the skater and skateboard spin for one complete circle, 360 degrees, usually on the ground. Most skater's can't do more than 360 degrees but Tony can. In fact he is famous for an amazing trick called a "900" where he spins 900 degrees - in mid-air!!

SPEAKING

Make a group of 3-4 students. Discuss the following topic:

There are many unusual hobbies and extreme sports on TV now. Think of the most interesting or unusual ones you've seen and tell the others in your group about it. If you have access to the internet, find some short videos of this sport or hobby to show everyone.

After everyone in your group has finished, choose the best one and present it to another group (or to the class).

WRITING: Let's Brainstorm and Go!!

With your partner, discuss your dream hobby or sport. If you could do anything you wanted without worrying about money, time, or danger, what kind of hobby or sport do you wish you were good at? Fill out the chart below, then use your notes to present to another pair.

Things that make me happy: _____

Questions	Your answers/URL
Hobby/sport we would like to be good at:	
Who are top people in this hobby sport?	
What points are exciting/cool about this hobby/sport?	
Interesting video of someone doing this hobby/sport:	

OPTIONAL PROJECT: Video Presentation

Work with a partner. Think of something that one or both of you can do well. Now create a short video to tell others about it.

Include at least a few sentences where you speak directly to the camera. If possible, also take some video of you showing what you can do.

As a class, watch the videos together and vote on your favorite.

CEFR GOALS SELF- EVALUATION	
I can use informal speech expressions such as "crazy."	1---2---3---4---5
I can understand and make comments about social media.	1---2---3---4---5
I can use vocabulary related to free time and hobbies.	1---2---3---4---5
I can identify and understand how modals (can/can't) are used.	1---2---3---4---5
I can express opinions regarding if free time activities are important or not.	1---2---3---4---5

Unit 5
Picnic Snack Ideas
\<Food\>

Learning Goals	Vocabulary and Grammar in the Video
Practical English: ● Speaking: Giving instructions to prepare food Critical Thinking: ● Considering and discussing the social value of picnics	Vocabulary: ● Food (ingredients) ● Verbs (cooking) Grammar: ● Countable and Uncountable Nouns

WARM UP: Talk about it

Look at the picture above. Work with a partner and answer the questions below.

● Have you ever gone on a picnic before? Talk about it.

● If you could go anywhere for your next picnic, where would you choose?

VOCABULARY: Matching

Match the words and phrases (1-8) to their definitions (a-h).

1. water _____   a. to make a liquid flow in a steady stream

2. cookie _____   b. to put something together with something else

3. mango _____   c. to press something firmly together

4. to crush _____   d. to make something look more attractive by putting things on it

5. to squeeze _____   e. a flat, round sweet baked bread

6. to pour _____   f. the clear liquid in seas, lakes, and rivers

7. to add _____   g. to damage something by flattening it

8. to decorate _____   h. a tropical fruit that is yellow inside

VIDEO: Predicting

Before watching the video, try to answer the following questions.

1. What foods do you usually buy when you go on a picnic?

_____

2. What snacks are easy to make for a picnic? Explain the recipe.

_____

VIDEO: Categorizing

Students must draw a line to match each ingredient with the Oreo Cheesecake or Mango Lemonade on Student Printout 1. One ingredient is included in both recipes!

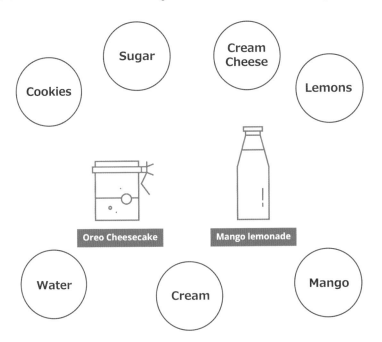

LISTENING: Comprehension

Watch again. Circle T for True and F for False.

1. You need 8 lemons for making the lemonade.   T   F

2. You have to boil the water so the sugar melts.   T   F

3. Big Oreo should be placed at the top.   T   F

4. You need to cut cookies into smaller pieces.   T   F

Dictogloss

Fill in the blanks by talking with your partners. Then watch the video to check your answers.

1. Hello everyone! Are you (   ) (   ) Mon's delicious picnic snack ideas? (0:12)

2. Then (   ) some (   ) (   ). (0:52)

3. Add your (   ) and (   ) (   ) (   )
   (   ) cream, and mix (   )! (1:00)

4. (   ) (   ) Mango Lemonade (   )! (2:23)

Focus on Countable and Uncountable Nouns

Narrator is talking about Oreos (0:33). Listen and fill in the blanks.

Cut half of them into bigger _____ and crush half of them into smaller _____. Then, you need _____ _____ and _____ _____ cheese.

DISCUSSION

Make a small group and discuss the following questions.

1. Do you like Oreos? What is your favorite way to eat them?

2. What kinds of picnic foods do you think would go well with Mango Lemonade?

WRITING: Critical Thinking

Why do you think people like to go on picnics? What is different about eating together at a picnic with eating at home or other places? Write a short essay with your opinion and bring it to class next time.

QUOTABLE QUOTES: Warm up

A picnic is more than eating a meal, it is a pleasurable state of mind.
  By DeeDee Stovel, famous author

Read the quote and then look at the picture. Do you always need to have a lot of food to have a good picnic? Explain.

VOICE DICTION: Video Shadowing

Start the video at 1:41 and (video counter) play one sentence by the narrator.

1) Fill in the blank with the missing words.

Cut (　　　　) (　　　　　) half, like this.

2) Watch the scenes and pronounce at the same time.
   Repeat several times until you can do it smoothly.

ROLE PLAYING: Natural Speech

Work with a partner. Pause the video after each stage of the Oreo recipe using the time code on the left. One of the students should name the ingredient, the other respond with the instruction for that ingredient. The first one has been done for you (Use the box below).

TIME	INGREDIENT	ACTION
0:38	Oreo	Cut half the Oreos/Crush the other half
0:50		
0:52		
1:00		
1:16		
1:18		

CRITICAL DISCUSSION

Make groups of 3-4 students. Read each essay one by one. Then....

● Choose the essay(s) with the most interesting ideas.
● Prepare to present those to the class in English.

READING: Awareness Raising - Prepositions

Find and correct the 6 errors in the essay below. Then listen to the CD to check your answers.

My family is always so busy that we never get to spend much time together. My brother

is always away for soccer practics or soccer matches and my Dad is often away on business trips. But last weekend all our schedules lined up and we were able to get away from Tokyo for the day to enjoy a nice picnic together. 5

My Dad loves the mountains and found a great spot under the river near Okutama, only about 2 hours to Tokyo.

It was a bit of a hike since the parking lot but at last we reached the river. The water was flowing quietly and 10 we came prior to a perfect spot just through a tree that could keep us towards the hot sun.

My Mom made us rice balls, fried chicken, french fries, and a whole bunch of Japanese sweets. Dad made a small fire and cooked up many different kinds of meats and vegetables. We ate, we swam, we talked, it was a wonderful day I won't soon forget! 15

SPEAKING

Think of 2 interesting places you went to for a picnic. Why did you enjoy it? One example has been given for you.

Place	Reasons
(e.g.) ABC park	Because we could make friends. We enjoyed taking playground equipment.

Make a small group. Introduce all the places each of you has been to, and then vote on the most exciting one. Then choose a spokesperson to introduce it to the class.

WRITING: Let's Brainstorm and Go!!

With your partner, discuss your dream picnic. Where would you like to go? What would you like to do? After that, write it down your whole plan and use your notes to present to another pair.

Place we would like to go: _____

	Notes
Things to do	
Things to see	
Things to eat	
How to get there	
Person(s) to go with	

OPTIONAL PROJECTS:

Choose one of the projects below. Be ready to show your results by next class.

Pair Work: Business

Imagine you are going to open a restaurant. Create a menu that includes starters, mains and desserts and present it in an A4 booklet.

Individual Work: Art and Media

Research a meal you would like to try or have tried only once. List ingredients and recipe stages. Then, practice presenting the recipe in the style of a cooking program. Use photos and props. Then take turns presenting the recipes. Once all recipes have been presented, vote on the meal you would most like to try.

CEFR GOALS SELF- EVALUATION	
I can talk about picnics.	1--2--3--4--5
I can infer meaning from context.	1--2--3--4--5
I understand what food for fun is.	1--2--3--4--5
I can use words about food.	1--2--3--4--5
I can use verbs about cooking.	1--2--3--4--5
I can clearly state my opinion about my dream picnic.	1--2--3--4--5

Unit 6
Volcano Adventure
<Technology>

Learning Goals	Vocabulary and Grammar in the Video
Practical English: • Speaking: Ability to talk about my dream job • Listening: Can listen for specific information Critical Thinking: • The growing importance of technology at work	Vocabulary: • Technology Words • Prepositions of Place Grammar: • Plurals

WARM UP: Talk about it
Work with a partner and answer the questions below.

- Who is the person in the picture?

- What do you think he is doing?

- Where do you think he is?

VOCABULARY: Matching

Match the words and phrases (1-8) to their definitions (a-h).

1. heat suit _____
2. drone _____
3. make camp _____
4. volcano _____
5. film (v) _____
6. virtual reality _____
7. lava _____
8. get dark _____

a. to set up tents and equipment for sleeping outside
b. a computer simulation of the real world which you can interact with
c. melted rock
d. the slow change from day to night
e. a small device that can fly and take pictures without a human pilot
f. to take a video of something
g. Special ouffits worn by people who work in very hot places
h. a large mountain that sometimes puts out smoke, fire and melted rock

VIDEO: Predicting

Before watching the video, make the class into 3-4 teams and try the following:

1) You have 2 minutes. Write the names of as many pieces of technology as you can on the board.
2) You have 2 minutes. Now write down as many jobs that require technology as you can.
3) Match the jobs and the technologies. Sometimes there is more than 1 answer.
4) Now try to predict:
  ● what the main character's job is _____
  ● which pieces of technology will be used by this person: _____
5) Check your answers after watching the video.

VIDEO: Sequencing

Now watch the video a second time. Check off the pieces of technologies you see or hear about in the video.

_____ laptop	_____ headphones
_____ drone	_____ camera
_____ GPS	_____ smartphone
_____ GoPro	_____ virtual reality headset
_____ stopwatch	_____ radar
_____ robot	_____ microphone

LISTENING: Comprehension

Watch again. Circle T for True and F for False.

1. Abrym is an island near Australia.   T   F

2. Sam takes a helicopter to work.   T   F

3. Sam flies in the drone to take pictures.   T   F

4. It's too hot for his smartphone to work.   T   F

Dictogloss - "get" collocations

Fill in the blanks by talking with your partners. Then watch the video to check your answers.

1. As he (   ) (   ), he sees that there's a lot of wind, and it's starting to (   ) (   ). (1:10)

2. We've gotta (   ) (   ). (1:22)

3. It's really exciting, but Sam needs to (   ) (   ). (2:10)

4. A heat suit. This suit helps Sam (   ) (   ), without (   ) (   ) (   ). (2:35)

Focus on Prepositions of Place

The narrator describes where Sam works (0:41). Listen and fill in the blanks

Ambrym is an island _____ the Pacific Ocean, _____ Australia. Ambrym has lots of volcanoes. Sam's job is to film _____ them.

DISCUSSION

Make a small group and discuss the following questions.

1. Make groups of 2-3 students.

2. Half the groups should brainstorm the advantages of Sam's job. The other groups should brainstorm the disadvantages of Sam's job. Answer the following questions:

   - How does technology help Sam to do his job?
   - Would you like to do a job like Sam's? Why/why not?

3. Now put together groups with each opinion and share your ideas.

4. Have a class discussion with each group presenting some key points.

WRITING: Critical Thinking

"People can't do their jobs without technology nowadays." Do you agree or disagree? Write a short essay with your opinion and bring it to class.

QUOTABLE QUOTES: Warm up

Choose a job you love, and you will never have to work a day in your life.

By Confucius

Look at the picture and the quote above. Think about this unit. What do you think it means?

VOICE DICTION: Video Shadowing

Start the video at 0:50 (video counter) and play one sentence by the narrator.

Watch the scenes and pronounce at the same time. Repeat several times until you can do it smoothly.

ROLE PLAYING: Natural Speech

Work with a partner. Replay the video from 01:22 - 01:24 "We gotta get started."

1. Repeat the sentence, copying the way that Sam says it.

2. Next, take turns making sentences about things you have to do after class, using 'gotta' in the same way as Sam.

example:

    A: What will you do after class?

    B: I gotta go to the bookstore. How about you?

    A: I gotta call my friend.

CRITICAL DISCUSSION

Make groups of 3-4 students. Read each essay one by one. For each essay:

- Write one question you would like to ask the writer.
- Write one suggestion to help them improve the essay.

Now, answer some of the questions. Your teacher may ask you to rewrite and expand your essay.

READING: Awareness Raising - Plurals

Find and correct the 8 errors in the essay below. Then listen to the CD to check your answers.

I think I have one of the best job in the world. Last year, when I was still a student at Leeds University, I was looking online for jobs and found a very unusual ad. It was a competition for a job with SplashWorld, to test out their many water slide. When I was growing up, I spent many ⁵ summer at waterpark with my friends and couldn't believe that I might be able to earn some money doing something I love so much.

The competition was hard. There were more than 2000 applicant. I was selected as one of 5 finalist. They flew us all to one of the water park ₁₀ in Egypt where we had to compete against each other. We did many interesting thing including having to make and sing a song while we went down the water slide.

I was lucky enough to win, so now I earn a salary of about 3,000,000 yen a year working full time for SplashWorld. They have more than 20 waterparks all around the world and they fly me to each park so that I can test and rate their water slides. I can't believe I get ₁₅ paid to do this. It's the greatest job in the world!

SPEAKING

In the US, many high school and college students earn extra money by doing "summer jobs." These are unusual and sometimes fun jobs that are done just for the summer months.

Make a small group. Introduce and discuss your "dream" summer job. Then choose a spokesperson to introduce the best ones to the class.

WRITING: Let's Brainstorm and Go!!

Work with a partner and brainstorm all the different technologies and software you have used over the past 24 hours. Work together and rank them in order of importance to you. Write down "why" each was important. After that, use your notes to present to another pair.

Rank	Technology / Reason why important	Rank	Technology / Reason why important

OPTIONAL PROJECT: Geography

Work with a partner. Research a country that has an interesting natural geographical feature, e.g. jungle/lake/river/waterfall/desert/mountain/volcano.

Find out at least three facts about that place, then discuss what technology you might need to explore its geographical features.

Next, each pair presents to the class the country they have chosen and which technology they would use to explore it.

CEFR GOALS SELF- EVALUATION	
I can speak about the growing importance of technology at work.	1---2---3---4---5
I can use technology words when speaking about jobs.	1---2---3---4---5
I understand "get" collocations (gotta).	1---2---3---4---5
I have a better idea about how to use plural -s-.	1---2---3---4---5
I can describe to others about my dream job.	1---2---3---4---5

Unit 7
Crazy Rides <Inventions>

Learning Goals	Vocabulary and Grammar in the Video
Practical English: • **Listening: Listening for numerical details in context** • **Speaking: Asking for specific information** Critical Thinking: • **What makes a good invention?**	Vocabulary: • **Transportation Words** Grammar: • **Past Simple (Irregular Verbs)**

WARM UP: Talk about it
Work with a partner and answer the questions below.

- How many kinds of transportation can you think of in 2 minutes? The pair with the most different types wins.
- Have you ever seen any crazy or very unusual cars or trucks? Talk about it with your partner.

VOCABULARY: Matching

Match the words and phrases (1-8) to their definitions (a-h).

1. houseboat ____   a. to ask someone to come to your house, to a party, etc.

2. ride ____   b. a vehicle with wings that can fly

3. tractor ____   c. to stay on the surface of a liquid and not go under things

4. plane ____   d. a small house that floats like a boat

5. to build ____   e. to arrive somewhere

6. to invite ____   f. to sit and control a vehicle or horse.

7. to float ____   g. to make something by putting parts together

8. to show up ____   h. a big vehicle with large back wheels that's used on farms for pulling things

VIDEO: Predicting

Before watching the video, try to answer the following questions.

1. What unusual thing do you think the car on page 45 can do?

_____

2. There is another unusual car shown in the video, what do you think it might be?

_____

Now watch the video and check your answers. Who was the closest?

VIDEO: Cloze Guessing

1) Read the sentences below and try to guess which type of word will go in each gap (number, noun, etc.)
2) Watch the video again and complete the gaps with the correct word.

● The tail used to come out another... I'd say ---------- inches. I had to cut that back...

● The vehicle took me about ---------- months to put together... it cost me a little under --------- dollars.

● Theon and his friends took the ---------- from the tractor and put them on the houseboat.

● About ---------- people show up for this thing and I'm there with a boat that may or may not float.

LISTENING: Comprehension

Watch again. Circle T for True and F for False.

1. Mark made a car into an airplane.   T   F

2. Mark takes his son to school.   T   F

3. Theon failed to make his car in the garden.   T   F

4. Many people came to see Theon's crazy ride.   T   F

Dictogloss

Fill in the blanks by talking with your partners. Then watch the video to check your answers.

1. And he (   ) (   ) make a (   ) lot of
   (   ). (0:43)

2. This (   ) (   ) me (   ) (   )
   months to (   ) together. (0:57)

3. Mark's so (   ) (   ) (   ) car, he wants
   to (   ) (   ) (   ). (1:19)

4. Woah! (   ) (   ) that (   )! (2:14)

Focus on Gerunds

The narrator is talking about Theon (1:33). Listen and fill in the blanks.

He likes _____ things too.

DISCUSSION

Make a small group and discuss the following questions.

1. Which of these "crazy rides" would you prefer to own? Why?

2. If you could make your own "Crazy Ride," which two types of vehicles would you
   put together and why?

WRITING: Critical Thinking

Why do you think people work so hard to customize their vehicles? The two people in this video are extreme examples but many people make changes to their cars and trucks. Write a short essay with your opinion and bring it to class next time.

QUOTABLE QUOTES: Warm up

*"The cars we drive say
a lot about us."*
By Alexandra Paul

Look at the picture and the quote above. Think about this unit. What do you think it means?

VOICE DICTION: Video Shadowing

Start the video at 0:43 and play one sentence by the narrator.

1) Fill in the blank with the missing words.

And he had to make (   ) (   )
(   ) (   ) changes.

2) Watch the scenes and pronounce at the same time.
   Repeat several times until you can do it smoothly.

ROLE PLAYING: Natural Speech

Work with a partner. Think of three questions with numerical answers you would like to ask Theon and three questions for Mark. Here are some examples.

● How long did the car take to make?

● How fast can it travel?

Next, one person pretends to be Mark and tries to answer the questions while the other gives the interview. Then, switch roles and try for Theon.

CRITICAL DISCUSSION

Make groups of 3-4 students. Read each essay one by one. For each essay:

● Write one question you would like to ask the writer.
● Write one suggestion to help them improve the essay.

Now, answer some of the questions. Your teacher may ask you to rewrite and expand your essay.

READING: Awareness Raising – Gerunds

Find and correct the 4 errors in the essay below. Then listen to the CD to check your answers.

The humble tuk tuk is a big part of Thailand's culture and at the heart of the Bangkok experience for most first-time visitors. The tuk tuk is a valuable method of transportation not only for tourists but also for locals and residents.

There's nothing like the buzz of take a spin around Thailand's capital in one of these open-air, 3-wheeled 5 vehicles which are the successor to the earlier human-powered 3-wheeled transport known as the rickshaw. In fact many people believe that the name tuk tuk comes from the sound the small engines make while buzzed through the busy streets.

Tuk tuks are generally safe and easy to use, but one important thing to remember while 10 walks around Bangkok is that you need to agree to the price before you get in. The driver will usually give a price that is too high and expect to bargain with you a bit. The price should be about the same as if you took a taxi. If you are worried, try check with someone at your hotel or at the airport about taxi prices and use that as your basis.

SPEAKING

Think of your favorite way to travel. Why do you like it so much? One example has been given for you.

Way	Reasons
(e.g.) Airplane	Because we can enjoy seeing our town from the sky.

Make a small group. Introduce your favorite way to travel, discuss each one, and then vote on which is the best. Then choose a spokesperson to introduce it to the class.

WRITING: Let's Brainstorm and Go!!

With your partner, try to think of a dream invention. Describe what it is and what it can do. After that, write down your plan and use your notes to present to another pair.

Your new invention: _____

	Notes
What is it?	
How can you use it?	
Who is it for?	
How you might make money with it?	

OPTIONAL PROJECTS: Car Design and Technology

As a continuation of the Video Follow-up Activity, you are going to design your own "Crazy Ride." In groups of four, try to think of innovative ideas for a new type of car. Then, agree on the best idea and draw up a design labelling the different features. The plan must include: what you want to make, what it will do, and what problems it will solve. Each group will present their idea to the class, and the class will then vote for the best idea.

CEFR GOALS SELF- EVALUATION	
I can talk about Crazy Rides.	1---2---3---4---5
I can infer meaning from context.	1---2---3---4---5
I understand what makes a good invention.	1---2---3---4---5
I can use the simple past.	1---2---3---4---5
I can use words about transportation.	1---2---3---4---5
I can clearly state my opinion about an invention.	1---2---3---4---5

Unit 8
The Climate Heroes
<Future>

Learning Goals	Vocabulary and Grammar in the Video
Practical English: ● Speaking: Solving real-world problems ● Listening: Connected speech Critical Thinking: ● Can children sometimes come up with better solutions to problems than adults?	Vocabulary: ● Environment ● Problems and Solutions Grammar: ● Time and Sequence Connectors

WARM UP: Talk about it

Work with a partner and answer the questions below.

● Who are the people in the picture?

● What do you think they are doing?

● What environmental problems are familiar to you?

VOCABULARY: Matching

Match the words and phrases (1-8) to their definitions (a-h).

1. wildfire   _____   a. to notice something that is partly hidden or not clear

2. rainfall   _____   b. power which comes from the sun or sunlight

3. fire brigade   _____   c. the amount of rain that falls

4. climate   _____   d. to invite someone to compete in a game or argument

5. solar energy   _____   e. people living in one particular area with a common interest

6. to challenge   _____   f. the weather conditions usually found in a particular place

7. community   _____   g. an organization that works to stop fires from burning

8. to detect   _____   h. a fire that is out of control in the countryside

VIDEO: Predicting

Before watching the video, try to answer the following questions.

1. What are the biggest problems in the world today?

_____

Write responses on the board.

2. Which one do you think will be the biggest problem in the future?

_____

Discuss these ideas as a class and try to reach and agreement.

VIDEO: Sequencing

Work with a partner. Look at the sentences below and discuss what you think the correct order is. Compare your answers with another pair. Then watch the video to check your answers.

_____   **The competition challenges young people to find solutions to climate problems.**

_____   **They won first place in regional and state climate competitions and selected to go to a world competition.**

_____   **Their project is called, Forest Guard, a system to detect fires as early as possible.**

_____   **Spain is our global connection because they have a similar climate.**

LISTENING: Comprehension

Watch again. Circle T for True and F for False.

1. The students choose fires as their problem.	T	F
2. The students want to visit Spain.	T	F
3. The students created a way for the public to help when there is a forest fire.	T	F
4. You need special training to become a Forest Guard.	T	F
5. The students didn't win the competition in Copenhagen.	T	F

Dictogloss

Fill in the blanks by talking with your partners. Then watch the video to check your answers.

1. The first (   ) that they want you to do is (   ) at: 'what is a problem in our community, (   ) to the climate?' (0:58)

2. Our (   ) (   ) is Spain because they have the same (   ). (1:28)

3. This (   ) the public (   ) be the forest guards, to keep our forests safe. (2:06)

4. Every group had an idea to (   ) a real (   ) using technology. (2:35)

Focus on Time and Sequence Connectors

Heidi teaches her students the three steps to find solutions (0:58). Listen and fill in the blanks.

1. "_____ that they want you to do is look at: 'what is a problem, in our community, related to the climate?'"

2. "_____ you have to find a global connection which is some place else in the world that has a similar climate to us or a similar problem."

3. "_____ you've done that they want you to think about a solution."

DISCUSSION

Answer the questions below with a partner.

1. What do you think about the students' Forest Guards ideas?
2. Does the video make you feel positive or negative about the future? Why?

WRITING: Critical Thinking

"Children are better than adults at solving problems." Do you agree? Write a short essay with your opinion and bring it to class next time.

QUOTABLE QUOTES: Warm up

"The world will not be destroyed by those who do evil, but by those who watch them without doing anything."
                    By Albert Einstein

Look at the picture and the quote above. Think about this unit. What do you think it means?

VOICE DICTION: Video Shadowing

Start the video at 1:08 and play one sentence by Tim.

1) Fill in the blank with the missing words.

This summer has been so terrible, (   )
the fires, (   ) I think we (   ) look
(   ) fires.

2) Watch the scenes and pronounce at the same time. Repeat several times until you can do it smoothly.

ROLE PLAYING: Natural Speech

Listening strategy: some words sound weaker than others

Replay the video section at 02:25 - 02:33 and complete the gaps using the first letter given.

O___ o__ t___ teams i_ f___ Australia, o___ i_ f___ Germany,
o__ i_ f___ Mexico City and o__ i_ f___ Idaho.

Speaking practice: repeat the segment, copying the way the speaker links the words together and paying attention to phoneme /ə/.

Make a similar sentence describing where your classmates are from.

CRITICAL DISCUSSION

Make groups of 3-4 students. Read each essay one by one. For each essay:
- Write one question you would like to ask the writer.
- Write one suggestion to help them improve the essay.

Now, answer some of the questions. Your teacher may ask you to rewrite and expand your essay.

READING: Awareness Raising – Time and Sequence Connectors

Find and underline the 6 time and sequence connectors in the passage below. Then listen to the CD to check your answers.

At the age of 16, Dutch teenager Boyan Slat was scuba diving in the ocean in Greece and was both surprised and sad that he saw more plastic than fish. After that, he began to think about how to solve this problem and eventually came up with an idea for a floating barrier that would collect the plastic using only the power of the ocean currents. Next, at the age of 18, he formed his company, "The Ocean Cleanup." Later, after 5 years of hard work, he built his first floating barrier known as "Wilson" in 2018. This barrier was then pulled out to a part of the ocean known as "The Pacific Garbage Patch," an area of the ocean, twice the size of Texas, which contains huge amounts of plastic waste. His next goal is to create at least 60 of these barriers with a target of reducing the amount of harmful plastic in the oceans by 50% by 2025. His ideas have inspired many to take action. If you are interested, look up his 2012 TEDx Talk to hear more about his vision.

SPEAKING

Make a small group and discuss the following:

1) What do you think about Boylan Slat's attempt to clean up plastic from the oceans?

2) What other problems can you think of related to our oceans and water supply?

Next, introduce the problems you thought of for number 2 and introduce them to the class.

WRITING: Let's Brainstorm and Go!!

In a small group of 3-4 students, research solutions to environmental/social problems, then choose the one you like best. E.g. Edible plates and forks/knives, machines used for removing plastic from the oceans/visitor tax to sites of natural beauty, etc.

Then design a campaign to promote your chosen solution. Create a poster, write a letter to investors, or prepare a presentation.

OPTIONAL PROJECTS:

Group Project: Media Literacy

Discuss which environmental problems you think are the worst. Choose one to focus on.

Work in groups to write a script and shoot a video to inform people about your chosen environmental problem.

CEFR GOALS SELF- EVALUATION	
I can talk about environmental problems.	1---2---3---4---5
I can discuss solutions to real-world problems.	1---2---3---4---5
I understand environment.	1---2---3---4---5
I can use time and sequence connectors.	1---2---3---4---5
I can vocabulary about problems and solutions.	1---2---3---4---5

Unit 9
A Different Kind of Journey <Travel>

Learning Goals	Vocabulary and Grammar in the Video
Practical English: ● **Speaking:** Recognizing and using contractions in natural speech ● **Listening:** Predicting content from visual cues ● **Writing:** Keeping a travel journal Critical Thinking: ● **Discussing the rewards of alternative travel.**	Vocabulary: ● **Travel** ● **Weather** Grammar: ● **Prepositional Phrases**

WARM UP: Talk about it
Work with a partner and answer the questions below.

● Have you ever traveled to any other countries in the world? (If not, where do you want to go in the future?)

● Do you enjoy traveling? Why or why not?

● What do you think this vicleo is about?

VOCABULARY: Matching

Match the words and phrases (1-8) to their definitions (a-h).

1. photographer _____   a. an area where people stay in tents for a short time

2. journey _____   b. a natural, fast movement of the air

3. travel _____   c. how hot or cold something is

4. camp _____   d. a unit for measuring temperatures

5. temperature _____   e. a trip from one place to another

6. degree _____   f. a portable house used by Mongolians

7. ger _____   g. someone whose job is to take photographs

8. wind _____   h. to make a journey

VIDEO: Predicting

Before watching the video, try to answer the following questions.

1. What do you think the video could be about?

_____

2. Where do you think it might take place?

_____

Now watch the video and check your answers. Who was the closest?

VIDEO: Sequencing

Work with a partner. Look at the sentences below and discuss what you think the correct order is. Compare your answers with another pair. Then watch the video to check your answers.

_____   **The Kazakhs have goats, cows, horses, camels and eagles.**

_____   **Timothy Allen is a photographer.**

_____   **The Kazakhs are travelling from winter home to summer home so that their animals have grass to eat.**

_____   **A ger is a Kazakh tent which stops the wind and the snow.**

LISTENING: Comprehension

Watch again. Circle T for True and F for False.

1. Tim is an ordinary photographer.   T   F

2. Gers are used for preventing the wind and snow from coming in.   T   F

3. On sunny days the temperature can be 40 degrees.   T   F

4. The Kazakhs would go on the long journey without the animals.   T   F

Dictogloss

Fill in the blanks by talking with your partners. Then watch the video to check your answers.

1. Timothy Allen is a (   ) who (   ) (   ) — but not like most people. (0:15)

2. He wants to do (   ) (   ) just see other cultures, he wants to (   ) (   ) them to really understand them. (0:23)

3. I'm really excited and I can't wait to (   ) (   ) (   ) (   ) now. (1:03)

4. One of the gers is (   ) and just (   ) (   ) (   ) (   ). (1:44)

Focus on Prepositional Phrases

The narrator discusses the travelers' period of stay (1:09). Listen and fill in the blanks.

For _____ five nights _____ _____ _____, the travelers sleep in Kazakh tents, called gers.

DISCUSSION

Make a small group and discuss the following questions.

What are the most important factors when taking a holiday? Discuss and rank the following 5 words in order from most important to least important. Then present your ideas to the class.

(   ) culture   (   ) weather   (   ) fun   (   ) hotel   (   ) relaxation

WRITING: Critical Thinking

Work in groups of 3-4 students. Imagine you are Tim Allen. Do you think he enjoyed the trip? What things were probably interesting? What things were hard?

Writing Task: You must work together to make a short journal book for Tim. One student writes about the first day of the trip, one about the second day, and so on until the final entry for the journal. Discuss it in your groups during class, write each journal entry at home, put the entries together into one journal, then show your journal to other groups.

QUOTABLE QUOTES: Warm up

"Two roads diverged in a wood and I.
I took the one less traveled by.
And that has made all the
difference..."

      By Robert Frost

Look at the picture and then read the quote above. Think about this unit. What do you think it means?

VOICE DICTION: Video Shadowing

Start the video at 1:03 and play one sentence by Tim.

1) Fill in the blank with the missing words.

> I'm really excited ( ) I can't wait
> ( ) get ( ) the road now.

2) Watch the scenes and pronounce at the same time. Repeat several times until you can do it smoothly.

ROLE PLAYING: Natural Speech

Work with a partner. Watch the scenes below. Pause the video at each place. Then role play what you would say if you were Tim or the woman in that scene. Use the language box to help you.

- 01:02 Tim describing his feelings

- 01:54 Tim telling us about the weather

- 02:34 The women's reaction to the view after arriving at their summer home

LANGUAGE BOX

- **Exciting!**
- **What a stunning view!**

CRITICAL DISCUSSION

Make groups of 3-4 students. Read each essay one by one. For each essay:

- Write one question you would like to ask the writer.
- Write one suggestion to help them improve the essay.

Now, answer some of the questions. Your teacher may ask you to rewrite and expand your essay.

READING: Awareness Raising - Prepositional Phrases

Find and correct the 10 errors in the essay below. Then listen to the CD to check your answers.

I grew up on a small town in New Jersey, on the east coast of the United States. It was a great place to enjoy the outdoors and was also close to some great beaches. But while in high school, I took a class with a history teacher that kind of changed my life. In that class she taught us in amazing places, cultures and countries from around the world, and when it was time to talk about Japan, she actually brought by an American university 5 professor who had lived there and could speak fluent Japanese!

At that moment, I knew I wanted to see the world, to expand my horizons. Almost none of my classmates were interested on anything outside with our hometown, so it was a dream I had to keep up myself until I graduated to college. A month after graduation I moved to Japan, my first foreign country. In the 30 years I have lived here, 10 I have traveled to more than 60 other countries, enjoying every one of them!

A few years back, I went to my 25-year high school reunion. Only 2 classmates out of several hundred had ever been abroad. All they wanted to talk with was last week's TV shows and how the local sports teams were doing. No one was interested on my travels, but I didn't care at all. My life and my journey have been magical, with each new place 15 opening my mind and my heart a little more. "Two roads diverged in a wood, and I took the one less traveled for, and that has made all the difference ..."

SPEAKING

Think of 2 unusual trips to other countries that you/friends/family visited. What was unusual about it?

Place/Country	Reasons

Make a small group. Introduce all the places/countries you or someone you know went, and vote on the most unusual one. Then choose a spokesperson to introduce it to the class.

WRITING: Let's Brainstorm and Go!!

With your partner, discuss your dream trip. Where would you like to go? What would you like to do? After that, write it down your whole plan and use your notes to present to another pair.

Country we would like to visit: _____

	Notes
What to do	
What to see	
What to eat	
How to get there	
Where to stay	

OPTIONAL PROJECTS:

Choose one of the projects below. Be ready to show your results by next class.

Group Project: Art and Media

Work in a small group. You must create a two-minute promotional video for a travel documentary you would like to make. The goal of the video is to convince the producers to pay for your trip and to make the documentary. Use photographs, narration, music and video recordings to make both the short film as well as a 1 page "treatment" explaining about the documentary you want to make.

Afterwards, each group plays their promotional video to the class, giving the other students a copy of their treatment and take questions regarding their film. Then, the rest of the class play the role of producers and votes on the film they would most like to see made.

Individual Project: Geography/ Information Literacy

Work in a small group. Research a remote "alternative travel" destination like the one in the video, and then find out how to travel there and what there is to do in that place. Then, create a presentation to show the class which includes the following information:

- Where the place is.
- How long it will take to get there.
- How much it will cost.
- Any special preparations travelers should make.
- What will be rewarding about the experience.

Present your ideas to the class and then the class will vote on the journey they would like to make.

CEFR GOALS SELF- EVALUATION	
I can talk about things like travel.	1---2---3---4---5
I can infer meaning from context.	1---2---3---4---5
I understand what travel means to everyday life.	1---2---3---4---5
I can have a better understanding of the prepositional phrases.	1---2---3---4---5
I can effectively use many words that are related to travel and. weather when speaking in English.	1---2---3---4---5

Unit 10
Chris, the Comic Book Writer <Literature>

CHRIS - THE COMIC CREATOR

Learning Goals	Vocabulary and Grammar in the Video
Practical English: ● **Listening: Predicting Content** Critical Thinking: ● **What makes a good story?**	Vocabulary: ● **Storytelling** Grammar: ● **Uses of Infinitive with "to"** ● **Relative Pronouns**

WARM UP: Talk about it

Work with a partner and discuss the questions below:

● Have you ever read manga or comic books?

● Which comic book hero is your favorite (this included movie versions)?

VOCABULARY: Matching

Match the words and phrases (1-8) to their definitions (a-h).

1. drawing _____ a. description of a series of events that people read for enjoyment

2. idea _____ b. someone who likes a famous person or thing very much

3. film _____ c. a magazine that tells stories in pictures with a small amount of writing

4. actor _____ d. someone who makes movies telling the actors what to do

5. fan _____ e. a suggestion or plan

6. director _____ f. a person who performs in plays, movies, or on television

7. story _____ g. a picture made with a pencil or pen

8. comic book _____ h. a story that is shown on a screen, usually at a movie theater or on TV

VIDEO: Predicting

Before watching the video, read the following questions and keep them in mind so you can answer them after the first watch.

1. Where is Chris from?

_____

2. What is the name of his hero?

_____

3. How many pages does the book have?

_____

Now watch the video and check your answers with a partner.

VIDEO: Sequencing

Complete the right column of the table with the different jobs each character has in the video.

CHARACTER	JOBS
Chris	
Thor	
Chris's Dad	
The Protector	

LISTENING: Comprehension

Watch again. Circle T for True and F for False.

1. Thor is a person who decides which comic books they sell.　　T　F

2. Chris failed to have the book ready in time.　　T　F

3. Plan B is to talk to another bookstore owner.　　T　F

4. Chris made the costume himself.　　T　F

Dictogloss

Fill in the blanks by talking with your partners. Then watch the video to check your answers.

1. His dream is (　　　　　) make his (　　　　　) comic book hero. (0:27)

2. I get (　　　　) ideas all the time, I can only (　　　　) his comic on the shelves if it's good enough. (0:52)

3. Chris has (　　　　) of making a comic book with his father his (　　　　) life. (1:31)

4. Chris (　　　　) Thor the story, shows him (　　　　) (　　　　), and explains his ideas for the film. (2:52)

Focus on the "to" Infinitive

The Narrator explains their conversation (0:56). Listen and fill in the blanks.

Thor needs ＿＿＿＿ ＿＿＿＿ the book ＿＿＿＿ ＿＿＿＿. Chris promises ＿＿＿＿ ＿＿＿＿ ＿＿＿＿ in two weeks.

DISCUSSION

Answer the questions below with a partner.

1. Based on what you saw in the video, what do you think The Protector is about?
2. Do you think you would like this story? Why or why not?

WRITING: Critical Thinking

What skills do you think might be necessary to be a good comic book writer? Write a short essay with your opinion and bring it to class next time.

QUOTABLE QUOTES: Warm up

"Inside each of us is a natural-born storyteller, waiting to be released."

By Robin Moore, author

Work with a partner. Look at the picture and the quote above. Think about this unit. What do you think it means?

VOICE DICTION: Video Shadowing

Start the video at 2:47 and play one sentence by the narrator.

1) Fill in the blank with the missing words.

(   ) (   ) did I make you a comic book, I made you (   ) film.

2) Watch the scenes and pronounce at the same time. Repeat several times until you can do it smoothly.

ROLE PLAYING: Natural Speech – Listening Strategies

Work with a partner. Watch the scenes below with no sound. Pause the video at the end of each scene and try to guess what they might be saying.

- 00:51 – 00:56
- 01:12 – 01:39

Now watch the video to check your answers.

CRITICAL DISCUSSION

Make groups of 3-4 students. Read each essay one by one. For each essay:

- Write one question you would like to ask the writer.
- Write one suggestion to help them improve the essay.

Now, answer some of the questions. Your teacher may ask you to rewrite and expand your essay.

READING: Awareness Raising – Relative Pronouns/ Infinitive with "to"

Find and underline the six "to infinitives" and the two relative pronouns. Then listen to the CD to check your answers.

Comic-con: What is it and why is it cool?

Where else in the world can you go to a convention and see superheros, wizards, spaceships and zombies all gathered in the same place? San Diego Comic-Con, which started in 1970 as a comic book convention with only 300 participants quickly grew to include science-fiction and fantasy films and TV shows and then expanded further to include almost every other genre including horror, anime, manga, card and video games and fantasy novels. By 2010 Comic-Con had reached the 130,000 person capacity of the San Diego Convention Center and has sold out every year since then. The event is so popular that a lottery  system is used to choose who will get tickets with all tickets usually selling out in just several minutes!

Comic -Con is a place full of exciting things to see and do. It gathers comic book writers, producers of superhero movies, science fiction TV shows and many other genres. It is a place for the fans to meet the stars and authors of these shows, a place to get a first look at trailers for the latest movies, and a place to dress up and celebrate people's love of a good story!

SPEAKING

Think of 2 interesting comic books you read. Why did you enjoy it?

Comic Book	Reasons

Make a small group. Introduce all the comic books you read and vote on the most exciting one. Then choose a spokesperson to introduce it to the class.

WRITING: Let's Brainstorm and Go!!

With your partner, discuss your dream hero. What does he/she look like? What are characteristics of the hero? After that, write it down your idea and use your notes to present to another pair.

A hero we would like to create: _____

	Notes
Appearance	
Characteristic 1	
Characteristic 2	

OPTIONAL PROJECTS:

Choose one of the projects below. Be ready to show your results by next class.

Pair Project: Literature

Make a pair. Write a comic version of this video. You must:

1. choose the important moments in the story.
2. decide on the style and layout.
3. think of how you can make the story as exciting as a comic book.
4. write/draw the comic book of the video.

Share your work with the class. Then take parts of each comic to make a complete class comic of the video.

Group Project: Life and Career Skills / Art and Design

In groups of three or four, prepare a pitch for a comic book idea and film adaptation for Thor. Create a film poster as support for your pitch. It should include a hero, a villain and a tagline or slogan for the film. Use your posters as support to pitch your idea to the rest of the class. Take a vote to choose the best idea.

CEFR GOALS SELF- EVALUATION	
I can talk about comic books.	1---2---3---4---5
I understand vocabulary about storytelling.	1---2---3---4---5
I understand how to create a new hero.	1---2---3---4---5
I can use relative pronouns.	1---2---3---4---5
I can use infinitive with "to."	1---2---3---4---5
I can clearly state my opinion about dream heroes.	1---2---3---4---5

Unit 11
Sharing Life with 1,000 Cats <People>

Learning Goals	Vocabulary and Grammar in the Video
Practical English: ● **Speaking:** Focusing on the gist ● **Listening:** Focusing on the gist Critical Thinking: ● **The consequences of helping others**	Vocabulary: ● **Numbers** ● **Animals** Grammar: ● **Past and Present Tenses** ● **Quantifiers**

WARM UP: Talk about it

Work with a partner and answer the questions below.

● Do you have any pets? If you could have any animal as your pet, what animal would you choose and why?

● Have you ever visited or seen any Cat Cafés in Japan?

VOCABULARY: Matching

Match the words and phrases (1-8) to their definitions (a-h).

1. animal _____
2. kitten _____
3. vet _____
4. pet _____
5. a cat person _____
6. rusty _____
7. pretty cool _____
8. online _____

a. good, fun or positive

b. when metal is old and changes to an orange color

c. an animal that someone keeps in their home

d. anything that lives and moves, including people, birds, etc.

e. someone whose job is to give medical care to animals that are sick

f. a young cat

g. something on the internet

h. someone who prefers cats to other pets

VIDEO: Predicting

Before watching the video, try to answer the following questions.

1. Where do you think Lynnea is?

_____

2. What do you think the video could be about?

_____

Now watch the video and check your answers. Who was the closest?

VIDEO: Numbers

Find a partner. Watch the video a second time, listening for any numbers you hear.
When you hear a number, write a short sentence that explains what the number is in the story.
Compare your answers with another pair. Then watch the video again to check your answers.

over 1,000	
30	
800	
300	
4,200	
1,600	
4 a.m.	
30 minutes ~ 1 hour	
500	

LISTENING: Comprehension

Watch again. Circle T for True and F for False.

1. Teresa comes to work at about four o'clock in the morning.   T   F

2. A vet visits Lynnea's house once a month to check animals.   T   F

3. Lynnea's job is to take care of her cats as long as possible.   T   F

4. Frank states that he likes dogs more than cats.   T   F

Dictogloss

Fill in the blanks by talking with your partners. Then watch the video to check your answers.

1. Lynnea ... she (   ) (   ) her own house (   )
   a business that (   ) (   ) cats. (0:12)

2. I went from a (   ) square foot, (   ) home with a
   pool and a view of the river, to a (   ), (   ) square
   foot mobile home with a view of a (   ) (   )
   (   ). (1:01)

3. We (   ) animals (   ) him every day (   )
   (   ) (   ). (2:18)

4. It may be (   ) (   ) (   )
   (   ) (   ), but Lynnea loves every single cat. (2:40)

Focus on Quantifiers

The narrator talks about The Cat House on the Kings (1:50). Listen and fill in the blanks.

There is _____ _____ to do every day, so _____ _____
_____ people work here.

DISCUSSION

Make a small group and discuss the following questions.
1. Could you live like Lynnea? Why or why not?

2. If you were to describe yourself as a pet, what would you be and why?

WRITING: Critical Thinking

What do you think of the following statement?

"It isn't good to have many animals in one place."

Decide whether you are for or against the statement. Write a short essay with your opinion and bring it to class next time.

QUOTABLE QUOTES: Warm up

"Happiness is a warm puppy."
By Charles M. Schultz

Look at the quote above. Think about this unit. What do you think it means?

VOICE DICTION: Video Shadowing

Start the video at 0:38 and play one sentence by the narrator.

1) Fill in the blank with the missing words.

(   ) opened 30 years ago (   )
(   ) 15 cats.

2) Watch the scenes and pronounce at the same time.
Repeat several times until you can do it smoothly.

ROLE PLAYING: Natural Speech

Work with a partner. Watch the scenes below. Pause the video at each place. Then role play what you would say if you were Lynnea, Teresa, or Frank in that scene. Use the language box to help you.

- 00:50 Lynnea showing him/her around her own house

- 01:31 Teresa telling us about what time do they usually start work

- 01:47 Lynnea describing a cat lying down in bed

- 02:00 Frank is happy about working at The Cat House on the Kings

LANGUAGE BOX

- **What a cute cat!**
- **I love cats!**
- **I'm so happy.**

CRITICAL DISCUSSION

Make groups of 3-4 students. Read each essay one by one. For each essay:

- Write one question you would like to ask the writer.

- Write one suggestion to help them improve the essay.

Now, answer some of the questions. Your teacher may ask you to rewrite and expand your essay.

READING: Awareness Raising - Past and Present Tenses

Find and correct the 10 errors in the essay below. Then listen to the CD to check your answers.

When I was growing up, I always have cats and dogs. They were a very important part of my life and each help me in a different way. My dogs were always cheerful, energetic and playful, ready to cheer me up whenever I needed it. My cats were not cheerful, energetic or playful (except when they are kittens), but were able to make me happy in other ways. When I would watch TV for example, my cat would often come and sit on my lap, purring with content, sometimes squeezing his claws into me to show he is happy. No matter how tough my day at school was, these pets always make me smile. 5

As an adult, I want to give my own children the chance to experience the same kind of 10 friendship and love that I got from pets and recently purchase a beautiful Australian Labradoodle named Aila. I know that owning a dog was a lot of responsibility and my daily life is much busier since we bought her, but truly she is worth the effort. Aila was a warm and playful dog with a silly sense of humor that makes us all smile or laugh 15 every single day. Though I buy her for my kids and take great joy in seeing the relationship Aila has with them, she has quickly become my best friend and I think I enjoy her every bit as much as my kids!

SPEAKING

Think of 2 interesting places you or your friends have been to play with animals. Why do you think it was interesting?

Place	Reasons
Penguin Bar Ikebukuro	Because we could enjoy playing with penguins. Plus, there are a wide range of food and drinks. The café is open until 4 a.m.!

Make a small group. Introduce all the places you went and vote on the most interesting one. Then choose a spokesperson to introduce it to the class.

WRITING: Let's Brainstorm and Go!!

With your partner, discuss your ideal pet café. If you could open up a store, what would you do with it? Where would be a good place to start? After that, write down your whole plan and use your notes to present to another pair.

My ideal pet café: _____

	Notes
Things to prepare	
Food menu	
Drink menu	
The appearance of the store	

OPTIONAL PROJECTS:

Choose one of the projects below. Be ready to show your results by next class.

Group Project: Business Studies

Research and create an idea for a new animal business.

First, research existing businesses such as animal shelters, pet sitters, and animal groomers. Then think about something else that animal owners might need or enjoy.

In the group, each member should take on a role for the new business and present your idea in the form of a Powerpoint to the class, explaining:

- What the business is and why it's needed.
- What it will cost for the customer.
- Who each of the team members are and what they will be doing within the business.

Other groups then vote on which business they like the most.

Individual Project: Art and Design

Lynnea has grown her business for over 30 years and is now very successful. Students should research a business or brand they admire and find out:

- When the company started.
- What their business does and where it is based.
- How many employees they have.
- What sort of jobs those employees do.
- What people like and dislike about working there.
- Whether the business or brand is famous for anything in particular.

Students then create an ad for a new job opening within the company. It should include information on what the job is and where, what the responsibilities will be, and why the person would love to work there.

CEFR GOALS SELF- EVALUATION	
I can talk about things like animals.	1---2---3---4---5
I can infer meaning from context.	1---2---3---4---5
I can understand the importance of helping other.	1---2---3---4---5
I can effectively use past and present tense.	1---2---3---4---5
I can clearly state my opinion about ideal cat cafes.	1---2---3---4---5

Unit 12
Living in 1927
\<History\>

Learning Goals	Vocabulary and Grammar in the Video

Practical English:
  ● Writing: identifying proper nouns and names
  ● Speaking: asking and answering questions about daily life
 	
Critical Thinking:
  ● Was life better or worse in the past?
	Vocabulary:
	  ● Homes
	  ● Entertainment and Technology
	
	Grammar:
	  ● have to

WARM UP: Talk about it

Look at the picture above. Work with a partner and answer the questions below.

● When you see this picture, what do you think of?

● What do you think she is doing?

VOCABULARY: Matching

Match the words and phrases (1-8) to their definitions (a-h).

1. to wash clothes _____   a. a place where people pay to watch films

2. bathroom _____   b. a machine used for accessing the internet and storing information

3. electricity _____   c. a room with a toilet and sometimes a bathtub and shower

4. heating _____   d. to make musical sounds with your voice

5. cinema _____   e. the system that keeps a building warm

6. phone _____   f. to clean something using water

7. to sing a song _____   g. energy that gives power to many kinds of devices

8. computer _____   h. a device used to talk to someone in another place

VIDEO: Predicting

Before watching the video, discuss the following in pairs:

Choose a decade in the past which you would like to visit. Then think of three reasons why and share them with the rest of the class.

VIDEO: Listening for Specific Information

Now watch the video a second time. Complete the 1927 column below.

	1927 (the 2nd year of Showa)	TODAY
Home		
Work		
Leisure		

Then, take a few minutes to complete the second column. Can you think of anything that people did in 1927 that we still do today?

LISTENING: Comprehension

Watch again. Circle T for True and F for False.

1. Their first morning living in the past is Deborah Griffiths' birthday   T   F

2. A fire in the kitchen is used for washing.   T   F

3. People in the past needed to be good at making things themselves.   T   F

4. The men go out together to play piano.   T   F

Dictogloss

Fill in the blanks by talking with your partners. Then watch the video to check your answers.

1. What d'you think you're gonna (   ) the most? (0:33)

2. They don't have (   ) and there is no bus so the men (   )
(   ) walk to work. (1:13)

3. (   ) is finished, so they think about having (   ). (2:06)

4. With no (   ) they have only candles to (   )
(   ) the night. (2:38)

Focus on "have to"

The narrator describes what they give to Deborah (1:49). Listen and fill in the blanks

It is not easy to buy presents, cards or cakes, so they _____ _____
_____ them.

DISCUSSION

In pairs, plan an interview with one of the characters in the series. Then, act it out, with one of student in the role of the character and the other in the role of interviewer.

WRITING: Critical Thinking

Play the video as many times as you need, and then write a report about life in 1927. Include as much information as you can, both from the video as well as additional information.

QUOTABLE QUOTES: Warm up

*A people without knowledge
of their past history, origin and
culture is like a tree without roots.*
By Marcus Garvey

Look at the quote above. Think about this unit. What do you think it means?

VOICE DICTION: Video Shadowing

Start the video at 0:26 and play one sentence by the narrator.

1) Fill in the blank with the missing words.

These people are going to live (   )
(   ) past (   ) (   ) TV show.

2) Watch the scenes and pronounce at the same time.
   Repeat several times until you can do it smoothly.

ROLE PLAYING: Natural Speech

In pairs or groups, choose one of the short conversations in the video and try to act out what might happen next.

CRITICAL DISCUSSION

Make groups of 3-4 students. Read each essay one by one. For each essay:

- Write one question to ask the writer for more information about a point in the essay.
- Write one suggestion to help them improve the essay.

Now, try to answer some of the questions. Your teacher may ask you to rewrite and expand your essay.

READING: Awareness Raising – have to

Find and correct the 3 errors in the essay below. Then listen to the CD to check your answers.

Have you ever been to a Renaissance Fair? If not, you don't know what you are missing! A Renaissance Fair is a big event where people has to dress up and speak as if they lived in old times, often as if it was England in the times of the Knights of the Roundtable or Henry the Eighth.

There are old style foods, drinks, and games, and of 5 course many cool old style things to buy.

To properly enjoy a Renaissance Fair, there are a few things you had to remember. The first, is to dress 10 properly. Have you ever wanted to dress up as a pirate, a knight, a maiden, a wizard or a Viking? This is your chance! Next, is how to speak. Many people try to imitate a British accent and the really dedicated fans, try to speak in Old English. You don't has to speak with an accent, but many people find this helps you get into the mood more. Finally, be sure to plan your day 15 well. Most Renaissance Fairs have many live events including Shakespearian plays, old-style comedies and even jousting contests with knights in armor fighting each other on horses. They are all free and shouldn't be missed!

SPEAKING

If you were transported back to live in the 1920s and could only take 1 item with you, what would it be?

Make a small group. Introduce and discuss your item, thinking about the pros and cons of each one. Then choose a spokesperson to introduce the best ones to the class.

WRITING: Let's Brainstorm and Go!!

With your partner, discuss advantages and disadvantages of living in the past. Think of at least two for each column, then use your notes to present to another pair.

Advantages	Disadvantages

OPTIONAL PROJECT:

Choose one of the projects below. Be ready to show your results by next class.

Individual work: History

Research what life was like in a decade of your choice in your home town or city. Try to find out as many details as you can and, if possible, find old photographs or illustrations. Based on that information, create a character in that time and start a personal diary. Every entry should cover a different aspect of life in that time (home, work, education, transport, family, etc.) This project can take the form of a blog and be carried out for just a few days or throughout the entire term.

Group work: Art and Media

Make a short video or a series of photographs (with titles) about life in a decade of your choice in the past. It can be narrative or descriptive but you must do your best to avoid showing anything that didn't exist at that time. Then present your work to the rest of the class. What elements were the hardest to hide?

CEFR GOALS SELF- EVALUATION	
I can speak about the living in the past.	1---2---3---4---5
I can use words about homes.	1---2---3---4---5
I understand how to use "have to."	1---2---3---4---5
I can describe to others about entertainments in 1920s.	1---2---3---4---5

Unit 13
Our Clothes <Clothes>

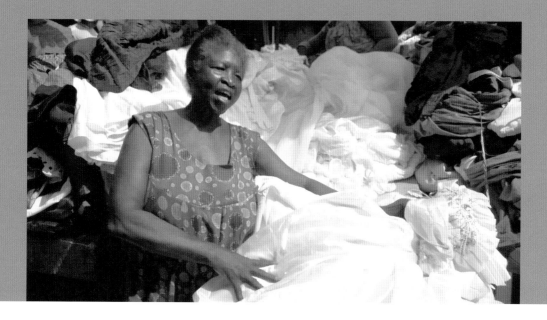

Learning Goals	Vocabulary and Grammar in the Video
Practical English: ● **Speaking: Discussion** ● **Writing: Article** Critical Thinking: ● **What to do with used or unwanted clothing**	Vocabulary: ● **Clothing** Grammar: ● **Relative Clauses** ● **Comparatives**

WARM UP: Talk about it

Work with a partner and answer the questions below.

● What do you think the video could be about?

● What do you think the woman in the picture is doing?

VOCABULARY: Matching

Match the words and phrases (1-8) to their definitions (a-h).

1. brand-new _____   a. to change from one thing to another new

2. second-hand _____   b. something used to make clothes flat and smooth

3. unwanted _____   c. not new; having been used in the past by someone else

4. trouser _____   d. to supply something at no charge

5. dye _____   e. completely new, not yet used

6. iron _____   f. not desired or needed

7. give away _____   g. something used to change the color of something

8. turn into _____   h. a piece of clothing that covers the lower part of the body from the waist to the feet

VIDEO: Predicting

Before watching the video, work with a partner and try to answer the following questions.

1. In what country or countries do you think this video takes place?

_____

2. What do you think the video will be about?

_____

Now watch the video and check your answers. Who was the closest?

VIDEO: Sequencing

Work with a partner. Look at the sentences below and discuss what you think the correct order is. Compare your answers with another pair. Then watch the video to check your answers.

_____   **Ade travels to the city.**

_____   **Ade visits a market.**

_____   **Ade meets people making changes to second-hand clothes.**

_____   **Ade travels to the countryside.**

LISTENING: Comprehension

Watch again. Circle T for True and F for False.

1. Ade Adepitan is traveling to Ghana to buy some second-hand clothes.   T   F

2. There are good quality clothes at the market.   T   F

3. Second-hand European clothes are more expensive than Ghanaian clothes.   T   F

4. In the mini factory, people can turn trousers into skirts.   T   F

5. Traditional Ghanaian clothing isn't important anymore.   T   F

6. In the city, local people don't wear Ghanaian clothing.   T   F

Dictogloss

Fill in the blanks by talking with your partners. Then watch the video to check your answers.

1. Ade Adepitan (   ) (   ) an adventure. (0:14)

2. So, what's (   ) (   ) here? (1:26)

3. You've got this guy here, (   ) (   ) dye
(   ) jeans, making old second-hand jeans look (   ).
(1:40)

4. Ade discovers ..., it's (   ) (   ) to be African. (3:13)

Focus on Auxiliary Verbs

Osei talks about the cultural importance of traditional clothing in Ghana (2:13). Listen and fill in the blanks.

There were _____ thet we _____ not read and write and so we were _____ our history in the clothes that we wear.

DISCUSSION

Make a small group and discuss the following questions.

1. What do you do with clothes you don't want anymore?

2. Do you just leave the clothes in the wardrobe?

3. Do you throw them away?

WRITING: Critical Thinking

In small groups, brainstorm the benefits of giving away the clothes you don't use anymore. After your group has generated three or four ideas, work individually to write a short article explaining these benefits. Bring it to class next time.

QUOTABLE QUOTES: Warm up

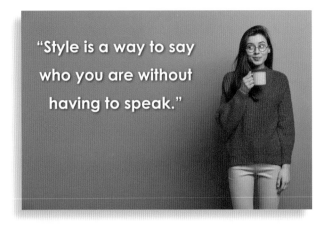

"Style is a way to say who you are without having to speak."

Look at the quote above. Think about this unit. What do you think it means?

VOICE DICTION: Video Shadowing

1) Start the video at 1:34 and (video counter) play one sentence by the narrator.

(   ) a guy just over there who's
(   ) trousers (   ) skirts.

2) Watch the scenes and pronounce at the same time. Repeat several times until you can do it smoothly.

ROLE PLAYING: Natural Speech

Work with a partner. Watch the scenes below. Pause the video at each place. Then role play what you would say if you were Ade, the customer, Osei Bonsu, or office worker in that scene. Use the language box to help you.

- 00:40 Ade's reaction to the best quality clothing that the salesperson showed
- 00:56 Customers 1 & 2 explaining why they only buy second-hand European clothes
- 02:11 Osei describing the reality of traditional clothing in Ghana
- 02:53 Office worker answering the question Ade asked

LANGUAGE BOX

– **I want to…**
– **It is cool to…**

CRITICAL DISCUSSION

Make groups of 3-4 students. Read each essay one by one. For each essay:

- Write one question you would like to ask the writer.
- Write one suggestion to help them improve the essay.

Now, answer some of the questions. Your teacher may ask you to rewrite and expand your essay.

READING: Awareness Raising – Relative Clauses

Find and underline the four "who" relative clauses in the passage below. Then listen to the CD to check your answers.

Do you like blue jeans? What's your favorite brand? Have you ever heard of, or bought a pair of Levis Strauss jeans? You might not know this, but Levi Strauss is actually the name of the person who invented blue jeans and his story is very interesting. Strauss was born in Germany in 1829 and came to America in 1853 to work for his brother who had a dry goods and clothing business. In 1849 a lot of gold was found in California, leading to the great California Gold Rush. Strauss was one of the many people who moved there, and it is here that he began making and selling clothes for the people who needed durable clothes for their work. His friend came up with the idea of putting strong metal rivets on the pockets and front of the jeans and Levi came up with the idea of using a denim fabric which he dyed dark blue to hide dirt and stains. The jeans became very popular among gold

A metal rivet on a pair of denim jeans

diggers, cowboys and others who worked outdoors. Levi Strauss chose the cowboy to market his jeans and with cowboy culture being so popular in Hollywood movies, by the 1930s, jeans also became popular as a daily fashion item, making Strauss a millionaire.

5

10

15

SPEAKING

Think of at least two clothes you would like to give away (anything is okay). Explain why. One example has been given for you.

Clothes	Reasons
(e.g.) jackets	There are too many jackets in my room. I don't have enough space.

Make a small group and discuss the following question: "How do you think the clothes you give away would be received in the market?"

WRITING: Let's Brainstorm and Go!!

Work with a partner and write a dialog for one of the following role plays. After you write it up, practice acting out the role play. Then try in front of the class.

Role-play 1
- Location: At a friend's house
- Situation: You and your friend are getting ready to go to a party and deciding what to wear.
- Participants: 2 friends

Role-play 2
- Location: At a local clothing store you know well
- Situation: the customer can't decide which clothes to buy and the salesperson tries to help
- Participants: 1 customer and 1 salesperson

OPTIONAL PROJECT:

Group Project: Social Studies Geography Business

Working in small groups, research and discuss what happens to other items that are given away (books, electronic goods, etc.). Then work together to make a poster or Powerpoint presentation to let your classmates know what you found.

CEFR GOALS SELF- EVALUATION	
I can talk about clothes.	1---2---3---4---5
I can infer meaning from context.	1---2---3---4---5
I can describe what I usually like to wear in English.	1---2---3---4---5
I can identify and understand relative clauses in English.	1---2---3---4---5
I can clearly state my opinion about clothes that are given away.	1---2---3---4---5

Unit 14
Food, Growing Cities
<Future>

Learning Goals	Vocabulary and Grammar in the Video
Practical English: • Listening: Focusing on a key issue when hearing about a complex problem • Speaking: Showing around Critical Thinking: • How to solve the problem of fresh food in big cities	Vocabulary: • Food • Cities Grammar: • used to

WARM UP: Talk about it

Work with a partner and answer the questions below.

- What do you think the term "Growing Cities" might mean?

- Have you ever tried to grow food by yourself? Share your memories of this.

VOCABULARY: Matching

Match the words and phrases (1-8) to their definitions (a-h).

1. desert _____
2. rooftop _____
3. grocery store _____
4. organic _____
5. neighborhood _____
6. garage _____
7. community _____
8. to grow _____

a. helping a seed develop into a full plant
b. a store where food and small household items are sold
c. the top surface of a building
d. a specific area where a group of people lives
e. not using artificial chemicals in the growing of plants and animals for
f. a large, hot, dry area of land with very few plants
g. a group of people that live near each other together
h. a building where a car is kept, often as part of a house

VIDEO: Predicting

Before watching the video, try to answer the following questions.

1. If you had to grow your own food, what would it be?

_____

2. Which cities in the US do you think might be trying to grow their own food?

_____

Now watch the video and check your answers. Who was the closest?

VIDEO: Checking

Before playing the video for the second time, look at the chart below and make a guess as to which sentences describes which city. Then, watch and check your answers.

	OMAHA	DETROIT	NEW YORK
1. In the past, people used to grow their own food very near the city.			
2. Most of what we grow now is not for people to eat.			
3. There are many unused spaces.			
4. Most people live in a food desert.			
5. They can buy junk food at grocery stores, but never have any fresh food.			

LISTENING: Comprehension

Watch again. Circle T for True and F for False.

1. Dan is from the U.S. but Andrew is from the U.K.   T   F

2. There are many unused spaces in Detroit.   T   F

3. They are using the empty space to sell the fresh food.   T   F

4. Green rooftops provide many benefits.   T   F

Dictogloss

Fill in the blanks by talking with your partners. Then watch the video to check your answers.

1. Changing the way (   ) (   ) (   ) today will change the way we (   ) our food ... (0:14)

2. They can buy (   ) (   ) at (   ) (   ). (1:24)

3. Back home, we also have (   ) (   ) (   ) that (   ) uses. (2:03)

4. But it's (   ) (   ) (   ) idea that some people (   ) it (   ) to believe. (2:37)

Focus on "used to"

Dan is talking about his hometown, Omaha (0:30). Listen and fill in the blanks.

People in Nebraska _____ _____ grow their _____ _____ very near the city.

DISCUSSION

Make a small group and discuss the following questions.

1. Can you find Omaha, Detroit, and New York on the map of the USA? Each student finds one of the places. Then show the map to the others and explain in English where it is while the others try to find the place.

2. Think about the words "food" and "space." Why are they important when comparing the situations in Detroit and New York?

WRITING: Critical Thinking

Which project – Brother Nature Farm or Brooklyn Grange – would work better where you live? Why? Write a short essay with your opinion and bring it to class next time.

QUOTABLE QUOTES: Warm up

"The greatest threat to our planet is the belief that someone else will save it."
By Robert Swan, Author

Look at the photo above. What is this place? Where is it located? How is the picture and quote related to this chapter?

VOICE DICTION: Video Shadowing

1) Start the video at 2:58 and (video counter) play one sentence by the narrator.

(　　　) there (　　　) green rooftops in our cities, there (　　　) be more fresh food and (　　　) air at the same time.

2) Watch the scenes and pronounce at the same time. Repeat several times until you can do it smoothly.

ROLE PLAYING: Natural Speech

Make a group of 4 and divide into 2 teams. One team will take on the role of Greg, who work at the Brother Nature Farm, and the other team will take on the role of Anastasia, who works at Brooklyn Grange. Each team member describes their farm to the other team, and tries to offer additional information to what they have seen in the video. You can use the video Transcript for inspiration.

LANGUAGE BOX

What is so special about our farm is …
Let me add one more point …
If you use our farm …
Our farm is different from something in that …

CRITICAL DISCUSSION

Make groups of 3-4 students. Read each essay one by one. For each essay:

- Write one question you would like to ask the writer.

- Write one suggestion to help them improve the essay.

Now, answer some of the questions. Your teacher may ask you to rewrite and expand your essay.

READING: Awareness Raising – used to

Find and underline the 3 examples of "used to." Then listen to the CD to check your answers.

Until recently, most tall apartment buildings used to be just boring square structures where all you could see was cement or glass. They used to use a lot of energy, a lot of water and made a lot of pollution. But if you go to Milan, Italy, you will see a pair of apartment buildings rising more than 100 meters in the air, which look and act very differently than other buildings. They are called the "Bosco Verticale" which translates as "Vertical Forest." Each tower is home to more than 900 trees, 5,000 shrubs and 11,000 plants, all of which work to do many good things such as cleaning the air from pollution and dust, producing oxygen, keeping the temperature inside the building stable

5

10

in both winter and summer, and even increasing the number of helpful insects and 15 birds. Until Bosco Verticale was built in 2014, all buildings in the area used to get their electricity from power plants and all water from the outside, but this building uses solar panels for renewable power and recycled water to water the plants, trees and flowers. Bosco Verticale is truly a remarkable building which not only helps us in the present but inspires us to build for a better future!

20

SPEAKING

Think of 2 interesting cities you visited. Why did you enjoy them? One example has been given for you.

Place	Reasons
(e.g.) Tokyo	Because people there are so nice. I also loved the delicious food.

Make a small group. Introduce all the places you went and vote on the most exciting one. Then choose a spokesperson to introduce it to the class.

WRITING: Let's Brainstorm and Go!!

With your partner, discuss your dream garden. What would you grow and what would it look like? Fill out the chart below, draw a picture if you like, then write it down your whole plan and use your notes to present to another pair.

Garden we would like to make: _____

	Notes
Things to grow	
What would it look like?	
Where to build	
Specialty	

OPTIONAL PROJECTS:

Choose one of the projects below. Be ready to show your results by next class.

Group/Pair/Individual Project: Biology

Working as a group, research 'urban gardening' and try to grow several plants. Working individually or in pairs to take care of your mini-gardens, writing about the process (profiles for each plant, watering plans, expectations, possible recipes, etc.) using simple language in a series of photo/video/audio/blog entries. Finally, make a presentation to talk about the project and to demonstrate/taste the results.

Group Project: Geography/Business and Entrepreneurial Literacy

Set up a business meeting. Looking at the map of the USA and – drawing an imaginary line for the road trip from Omaha to Detroit to New York – Think about what other major cities would be on Dan and Andrew' route. Working in small groups, research the climate of these cities and choose a city to support with your own ideas for a fresh food business. Each group prepares a presentation for a business meeting where they need to convince the 'investors.' Here are some points to consider: type of food, competitors in the area, help to the community.

CEFR GOALS SELF- EVALUATION	
I can talk about growing cities.	1---2---3---4---5
I can infer meaning from context.	1---2---3---4---5
I understand the problem about food in big cities.	1---2---3---4---5
I can use "used to" in my essay.	1---2---3---4---5
I can show my partner around using phrases I've learned.	1---2---3---4---5
I can clearly state my opinion about dream garden.	1---2---3---4---5

NOTE

NOTE

Expanding Horizons: [B-906]

Critical Thinking through Authentic Video <CEFR A1-A2>

世界を巡る映像で学ぶ総合英語〈基礎〉

第 1 刷　2020 年 3 月 16 日
第 4 刷　2023 年 3 月 31 日

著　者　チャールズ　ブラウン　　Charles Browne

田邉祐司　　Yuji Tanabe

発行者　南雲一範　Kazunori Nagumo
発行所　株式会社　南雲堂
　　　　〒162-0801　東京都新宿区山吹町361
　　　　NAN'UN-DO Publishing Co., Ltd.
　　　　361 Yamabuki-cho, Shinjuku-ku, Tokyo 162-0801, Japan
　　　　振替口座：00160-0-46863
　　　　TEL: 03-3268-2311（営業部：学校関係）
　　　　　　　03-3268-2384（営業部：書店関係）
　　　　　　　03-3268-2387（編集部）
　　　　FAX: 03-3269-2486

編集者　加藤　敦
組版・印刷　啓文堂
装　丁　銀月堂
検　印　省　略
コード　ISBN978-4-523-17906-1　　　C0082

Printed in Japan

落丁・乱丁，その他不良品がございましたら，お取り替えいたします。

E-mail nanundo@post.email.ne.jp
URL https://www.nanun-do.co.jp/